Self-Esteem:
The Power to Be Your Best

Written by Mark Towers
Edited by National Press Publications

NATIONAL PRESS PUBLICATIONS
a Division of Rockhurst College Continuing Education Center, Inc.
6901 West 63rd Street • P.O. Box 2949 • Shawnee Mission, KS 66201-1349
1-800-258-7246 • 1-913-432-7757

National Press Publications endorses non-sexist language. However, in an effort to make this handbook clear, consistent and easy to read, we've used the generic "he" when referring to both males and females throughout. The copy is not intended to be sexist.

TABLE OF CONTENTS

1

WHAT IS SELF-ESTEEM AND WHY IS IT ESSENTIAL TO US?

How many times has this happened to you? You are faced with a challenge — winning a marathon, taking first place in a writing competition, getting a promotion. And then it happens, you win, you get promoted!

And guess what happens next? You say to yourself, "this doesn't mean that much...those judges weren't that qualified...the other runners weren't in very good shape...well, who else would they promote? The job's not that great." In other words, you tell yourself, "I won, but I don't feel like a winner."

No matter how many times you succeed, your accomplishments can't touch that person inside. And that's where it counts, because that's where you really live after all the fanfare dies down — inside your mind. So, what's it like in there, anyway?

If you look closely, you'll see the little child you were so many years ago. That little child may have some qualities that blossomed as you matured: wisdom, humor, strength of purpose, the ability to communicate well with others. No doubt that child is also like most other children — at times fearful, unsure, dependent on adults to know what to do and unaware of his own special qualities.

We'll work more with your own inner child at a later point, but for now you should know that within that early version of yourself lies the seed of your self-esteem. Without understanding how certain childhood patterns may have evolved into adult behavior, you cannot build a strong sense of self-esteem and confidence. Self-esteem is not something you can graft onto the tree of a full-fledged adult personality. You must go back and find a young branch of your impressionable childhood from which self-esteem can sprout and flourish.

What Is Self-Esteem?

Self-esteem means truly loving and valuing yourself. This is quite different from being an obnoxious, overblown egomaniac who is always telling other people how great he is. Often the people who brag the loudest are those most desperately lacking in true self-esteem.

Good self-esteem means you have accepted yourself as you are. It means you are still working to improve yourself, and while that process is taking place, you have a healthy appreciation for yourself, your best qualities and your finest achievements.

Self-esteem acts as a conduit through which all our aspirations and goals can pass into real, achievable results. It means we accept and care about the person we are today.

To determine if your self-esteem is healthy and in good working order, ask yourself the following questions:

1. *Do I accept myself for what I am?* That includes your looks and feelings, your strengths and weaknesses. Do you accept your feelings when you're angry, frustrated or depressed, as well as when you're joyful and productive? Learning not to deny your feelings is an important part of

developing good self-esteem. Listen to how you talk about yourself. Are you constantly putting yourself down? This can send a negative message to your subconscious that you believe you truly don't deserve the best in life. Maybe it's time to start focusing on your strengths while you try to correct your weaknesses.

2. *Do I give myself credit for what I do?* When people ask, "What do you do?" do you feel apologetic and defensive, murmuring, "Oh, I'm just a secretary/accountant/ housewife/salesman."? It's tough in today's world not to feel like we're failures if we're not multi-millionaires or celebrities. But stop and think a moment about all you do in a day. It helps if you make a list. You clean your house, care for your children, prepare meals, go to a job and work with others, perhaps you care for elderly parents and — on top of all this — still participate in community and social life. That's a lot to be proud of. Once you accomplish a goal, do you give yourself credit?

3. *Do you take time out to recognize your hard work?* Your accomplishments? Or do you still feel you don't quite measure up? Have I developed my own values? Maybe we unquestioningly incorporated our parents' values: that every daughter should be married with three children; that every son should be earning an annual salary of $50,000 or more. Or perhaps we've adapted to acceptable social stereotypes: that women should be polite and submissive, putting other people's needs before their own; that men should be aggressive breadwinners, suppressing their feelings. It's important to know what's right for you and you alone. See if you've compromised your values by trying to meet the unrealistic standards of others or by accepting behavior you really don't condone. If you live only to meet others' expectations, you'll never meet your own.

4. *Can I turn setbacks into victories?* Successful people, it is said, see problems as opportunities. Unsuccessful people see opportunities as problems. It's all in your point of view. Don't let your plan for success get short-circuited by negative experiences. We often learn more about

ourselves through failure than we do with success; we learn about our limitations, how we react to stress, where our true priorities are. Look at what you learned from your latest setback. Perhaps you know how to better manage your co-workers now; perhaps you understand a technical function of your job you never knew before; perhaps you know that, because your kids were in trouble, now they need your help.

It's important to remember that temporary setbacks are no reflection on you or your abilities. They don't redefine you as a weak, incompetent person. Setbacks occur in everyone's life. How you turn them to your advantage is up to you.

Good Self-Esteem Means a Healthy Self-Image

A self-image doesn't come from the mirror, it comes from within. Lack of self-esteem is like being psychologically anorexic. No matter how thin you are, you look in the mirror and see the same overweight/unacceptable person. Are you perpetually dissatisfied with yourself, no matter how much you diet and exercise? Or are you a chronic overachiever, always belittling your latest success and thinking you'll be fulfilled by the next challenge?

Perhaps the problem stems from trying to be someone else, to live someone else's life and not your own. A poor self-image is like looking in a cloudy mirror that always reflects back the same unacceptable person to us, no matter how many external changes we make.

Ask yourself these questions to see if your self-image could use some polishing:

1. *Do I constantly fantasize about what my life will be like after I've*:

   • Lost 20 pounds?

   • Joined a health spa?

   • Met the right partner?

   • Bought a new house?

   • Bought a new car?

Guess what. Your life is happening right now and it can't wait. Learn to make the most of your immediate opportunities by learning to value yourself as you are at this moment.

2. *Am I a perfectionist? Do I:*

- Continually refine my work so that everyone will think it is "perfect?"

- Expect others to do the same? If they don't, do I judge them unfavorably?

- Believe that my hair and clothes should always be immaculate — regardless of the circumstances?

- Avoid taking risks because I could end up looking foolish?

As a perfectionist, you may be valued by others because they know they can depend on you to do a great job. People with high self-esteem certainly care about their work and appearance. Yet excessive concerns that result in perfectionism — being intolerant of ones own or others' mistakes — can mean that your self-image is dependent on others' opinion of you.

3. *What is my body language saying about me? Do I:*

- Walk around with slumped shoulders?

- Avoid making eye contact with others?

- Hug my body in a protective way?

- Experience chronic low energy?

- Endure chronic backaches, shoulder aches or other discomforts as a result of tension?

How you sit, stand and speak tells the world a lot about how you feel inside. This may sound like an old adage from your Aunt Mildred, but it's important to relax your shoulders, stand tall and erect. Your upright posture tells others that you have pride and confidence in yourself. It also allows you to breathe easier and more efficiently. You'll feel better immediately by increasing your oxygen intake.

Chronic fatigue can indicate a real medical problem. If it persists, you should consult a doctor. However, it can also be a symptom of depression and defeatism. When your brain is filled with negative thoughts, your body eventually refuses to get into gear.

If, after answering the questions above, you think your self-image could use some improvement, realize you're not alone. Advertising has taken its toll on our self-esteem. We're constantly bombarded by messages from the media, as well as from real life, telling us it's easy to be richer, thinner, younger, more successful, more sexually attractive, more socially accepted. These achievements, of course, are linked to external, material solutions. We're convinced others will find us fascinating if we use expensive moisturizers, drive certain cars, wear the right clothes or perfume, or work out at celebrity-packed health clubs.

Getting in Shape Versus Becoming Obsessed with Weight

Everyone wants to be healthy and fit. There's nothing like the confidence and sense of well-being that follows a vigorous work-out or fast-paced walk. By exercising regularly, we not only shed pounds and develop muscles, but our bodies become fun to live in once again, responsive, flexible and strong.

How you feel physically is certainly a big part of your self-esteem and self-image. But just because a person is in shape doesn't mean he doesn't suffer from self-doubt, fear or depression like everyone else. Unfortunately, our body-conscious society prefers to focus on externals, glamorizing beautiful stars and sports heroes over philosophers and physicists. Therefore, it's easy for us to be continually dissatisfied with how we look because it's one of the major ways in which we're judged.

Women, especially, link body-image to self-esteem. It may come as a surprise to learn that some of the world's most successful women have suffered from a poor self-image. Maria Callas, one of the great sopranos of the 20th century, was obsessed with the idea of looking like Audrey Hepburn, whom she had seen in the movie, "Roman Holiday." At great risk to her health, she quickly shed 80 pounds so that she would appear more glamorous both on and off stage. Some critics feel Callas' voice was never the same after this tremendous weight loss.

In the beginning of her career, Jane Fonda resorted to the most common remedies to quickly lose unwanted pounds: starvation through obsessive dieting and laxative abuse that led to bulimia and anorexia. It wasn't until Fonda discovered alternatives through proper eating habits and regular exercise that these destructive habits were overcome.

Oddly enough, a thinner you doesn't always mean a happier you. A recent study of 682 coeds in a Midwest university revealed a clear relationship between eating disorders, unhealthy behavior to control weight and diminished self-esteem. The researcher reported the damaging effect of American society's "pervasive preoccupation" with female weight and appearance being linked to greater vulnerability and depression.

Although the study was evenly divided between men and women averaging 19 years old, the body-image/self-esteem relationship was considerably greater among the women. Women wanted to weigh less, while men wanted to be more muscular and weigh more. Even when the subjects fell within a normal weight range, the women tended to consider themselves ten pounds overweight, while the men tended to consider themselves only three pounds overweight.

As everyone knows, fad diets are destructive because they don't work. In the process, the diet:

- Eliminates fat, but also consumes a certain measure of muscle.

- Lowers metabolism.

- Provides inadequate nutrients in imbalanced combinations.

- Taxes the entire body, making some dieters subject to congestive heart failure and strokes.

- Ensures that the dieter gains fat more quickly once the diet has ended.

Becoming obsessed about your weight is also detrimental to your psychological health because you:

• Internalize the standards of others as to what is attractive.

• Emphasize how you look over how you feel.

• Are kept in a vicious cycle of weight loss followed by unavoidable weight gain once you are off the diet.

• Perpetuate negative emotions like self-disgust, frustration, anger.

• Damage your self-esteem.

So what's the answer? Are you meant to go through life a hopelessly fat, underachieving slob? Absolutely not! By building from the inside out, rather than from the outside in, you'll gradually begin to look the way you want to look, but you won't give up any part of yourself in order to have it.

In the next few chapters, we'll examine what poor self-esteem and a negative self-image can do, and then how to counteract these destructive patterns. We'll also talk about defining and achieving goals and their importance in your life. Finally, you'll want to know how to build self-esteem in others. We'll talk about how to affirm, not deny, your own inner child's feelings and deal more effectively with your family as a whole.

Remember, self-esteem is a precious gift you can share with anyone. By understanding and communicating good self-esteem, you can have a supportive, inspiring influence on others as they make their journey through life.

The following is an exercise that will get you off to a good start in building self-esteem. Similar exercises will appear at the end of each chapter. You'll want to keep a spiral notebook or personal journal to note your reactions as you work through these exercises.

EXERCISE NO. 1: SELF-ACCEPTANCE

For this exercise you must have a hand-mirror. Take a deep breath and close your eyes. Concentrate on you. Think of how you look in the full-length mirror when you're dressing in the morning

— with all the imperfections, bulges and saggy places. Don't try to superimpose a sleeker image — like how you'll look after 30 aerobics classes. Just concentrate on the present, how you look and feel. Keep your breathing regular and relaxed. Imagine your image in the mirror surrounded by a halo of shining light. This radiant light emanates from your innermost being, it's filled with love and healing energy. See it pulsating all around you. It feels warm and caressing. Now slowly open your eyes and look into the hand-mirror. Looking into your own eyes, say these words, "I love and accept you exactly as you are." When some people do this exercise they feel calm and happy. Others start criticizing the person they see in the mirror. Suspend all critical thoughts. It's okay if you feel frightened or sad. Just look into your eyes, and repeat, "I love and accept you exactly as you are." What do you feel now? Take out your notebook and write down your reactions. Listen for negative thoughts, resistence and self doubt. Repeat this exercise daily. At the end of three weeks, check your notes. Can you see a pattern of greater self-acceptance developing? Does the exercise become easier over time? Are there days when it's harder to do? If so, why? Are you experiencing greater stress on those days? Realize that the way you feel about yourself can often be triggered by an outside event — that your own inner sense of self-esteem can gradually become removed from any negative stimuli.

SUMMARY

Self-esteem means loving and valuing yourself. It is a way to connect today's dreams with tomorrow's realities by ensuring real, achievable results.

People with good self-esteem accept themselves as they are, give themselves credit for what they do and know how to turn setbacks into victories. They live by their own set of values.

Good self-esteem is linked to a healthy self-image that reflects a strong, vibrant energized person. People with poor self-esteem often have a negative self-image that can cause them to:

- Not seize upon today's opportunities. To constantly fantasize about doing things "tomorrow," which never comes.

- Become perfectionists, obsessed by their appearance and by doing things "right".

- Communicate their negative self-image through poor body language.

Self-esteem is an important ingredient in improving not only your life, but the lives of everyone you contact. It can make everyone's journey of self-discovery smoother, more pleasant and more fulfilling.

2

WHEN SELF-ESTEEM
IS LACKING

How well we accept and judge others is a pretty good indication of how well we accept ourselves. When self-esteem is poor, we're often critical and judgmental of others. In fact, it's our own self-image that we're really unhappy with.

We might take a secret pride in thinking of ourselves as being very discriminating, making the excuse that we have "high standards" or that we're hard workers and expect others to be. If our friends and co-workers accuse us of being overly demanding, we might reply with the slightest trace of condescension, "I guess I'm just a perfectionist." Inside we are thinking, "I can't help it if I'm tough on others. I want the best!"

Be the Best. . . or Else!

Unfortunately, such judgmental attitudes are often a replay of the unrealistic expectations our parents placed on us as children. They're psychological burdens we've carried around all these years and we dump them on the first unsuspecting parties we find — our children, our marriage partners, our fellow employees, our best friends.

Do you use a lot of words derived from parental role-models: should, ought, mustn't? Do you use phrases like, "listen to me," "I wouldn't do that if I were you," "I simply can't stand it when..."? Basically, if we don't respect ourselves we often seek it or demand it from others — a classic symptom of low self-esteem.

The Price of Workaholism

Workaholism and perfectionism are other symptoms of low self-esteem. Both types of behavior indicate personalities that are externally driven, rather than internally driven by self-defined goals. Workaholism and perfectionism are difficult addictions to spot because they're condoned in the workplace which often values long, hard hours over personal happiness.

However, the devastating effects of workaholism on our family lives can no longer be ignored. When allowed to flourish unchecked, it can lead to drug and alcohol abuse, emotional co-dependency, divorce and physical abuse.

To find out if you're working too long and too hard, ask yourself the following questions:

1. *How many hours a week do I spend at my job?* How much time your job requires depends on your position, of course. But no matter whether you're a vice president or an administrative assistant, some people choose to work ten hour days as well as on weekends. Out of middle managers, 21 percent spend between 41 and 49 hours per week at their jobs; and 53 percent spend 50 to 59 hours. The rat race doesn't slow down as you move up. Most high level executives (58 percent) spend 50 to 59 hours a week working; while 29 percent put in 60 to 69 hours. The question is, is all the sweat necessary?

2. *Do I choose to work these hours or does my company expect me to?* Most workaholics begin by being externally driven. You may find yourself working for a company that expects you to put in "12 hours — from 8 a.m. to 8 p.m." But Fortune 500 companies are wising up. They are beginning to understand that long hours lead to employee burnout and lessened effectiveness on the job. Some commentators even feel that employees who spend all day and most of the evening at the office are not necessarily a boon to the company. Says one Sara Lee executive, "I think it's absurd for people to be divorced from the community."

3. *Can you lessen the hours you spend at work without putting your job in jeopardy?* Before you react with a resounding "No!", think about ways you can improve performance, get more done in less time, and still leave at 5:30 by doing the following:

   - Limit time spent socializing that interferes with getting the work out.

   - If you're trapped in unproductive meetings, ask an attendee to take notes for you or record the meeting.

   - Opt for flex time, or work through lunch to make your day shorter. Vary your routine. Getting out of the rut of working the same hours can be energizing.

   Some executives who have trimmed their work weeks to 40 hours find they're much more productive. They work just as hard as ever, but the hours are more reasonable. Try it; you might be surprised by the results.

4. *Do you have a well-rounded life?* How much time do you spend with your children, on community projects and church groups?

When both you and your spouse have careers, your children might be getting lost in the dust of the fast track. The same social pressures that force you to appear strong and committed at work also exist for your children. They must keep up in school and avoid becoming drug abusers, teenage moms or high school dropouts — often with only minimal support from their parents. Ask yourself:

- How much time do I spend helping my school-age children with homework each night?

- Am I available on week nights or on weekends for intramural sports/theatre events or girl scout/boy scout meetings?

- Even if my time is limited, do I make an effort to spend time with my child — say, special monthly outings at the zoo, children's theatre, movies?

- Do I make time to visit my child at school? Children take pride in their parents attending school plays and field days; joining them for lunch; helping out at pancake dinners. Some parents can become "visiting resources" — discussing what they do for a living with their children's classrooms.

5. *Do you have time for yourself?* The more fun you're having, the more fun you are to be around.

- Try taking a class in scuba diving or archaeology. Go on a dig and sift some dirt. Or just lie around the beach, soaking up the sun and relaxing.

- What about hobbies and recreation? When was the last time you took an aerobics class, swimming lessons, or tuned that old guitar you used to strum? Find something you like to do and weave it back into your life.

- Do you schedule time to spend with community or social groups you enjoy? Maybe you're interested in gardening, recycling, or getting city hall to build new sidewalks in your neighborhood. Becoming part of a community action group can increase your awareness of local issues. By participating, you reap the rewards of getting things done and increase your sense of personal effectiveness outside the office.

- When was the last time you had lunch with an old school chum whose wacky outlook on life refreshed and recharged you? Make time for the people whose company you truly enjoy.

- Do you take regular vacations? Vacations can threaten workaholics who are afraid the office will cease to exist if they're not there every single day. Actually, they're probably more afraid of the void of unplanned time and plunging into the unknown. Start by taking just a little time off and see what happens at the office. They never knew you were gone, right? You had fun getting away, and now it's fun to come back to work. Everybody wins!

When Your Worst Enemy Is You

Sometimes our criticalness turns inward and we pronounce harsh judgments against ourselves. No matter how much we strive, we continue to feel inadequate and weak, constantly comparing ourselves to others. We're not as thin as Cher, we're not as rich as Elizabeth II, we're not as strong as Arnold Schwarzenegger. And we're certainly not as outgoing as that new assistant manager they just hired in the Production and Development Department.

Comparisons are a waste of time because no two people are alike, with the same abilities and interests. We can always find people to compare ourselves to — who make us look pretty good or downright awful. When your self-image doesn't measure up, your friends may be offering you some perspective with the following advice:

"You know, you are your own worst enemy."

"You're harder on yourself than you are on others."

"You expect too much from yourself. Learn to take one day at a time."

If everyone's telling you to give yourself a break, try doing it! For two or three days pretend not to care if the bath towels are straight and centered on the towel racks. Try to ignore that inner voice that says you're a bad housekeeper, an indifferent parent, an uncaring spouse. Don't be surprised if you feel guilty or scared or sad. Changing your behavior can be threatening.

If lightening up isn't easy, you might want to take a look at the behavior patterns you learned a long time ago.

When Others Seem to Have It All

Watch children at play sometime and see if you observe them "acting like adults." Most likely, they're acting greedy or selfish, screaming from the top of the jungle gym or totally absorbed in filling their pail with sand from the sandbox. In other words, they're acting just like children. Just like you did once. Remember?

Children have an almost endless ability to play, to invent, to create, to dream. These pastimes are not so much the products of thinking as they are of feeling. Unless they're the victims of abuse, younger children are very in touch with their feelings. Socialization comes later, when they absorb adults' teaching of certain feelings as "bad" or "unacceptable."

Letting feelings out naturally and spontaneously is what children do best. By squalling, a baby tells the world in no uncertain terms what it feels like to have a wet diaper or to be hungry; by scuffling and yelling, children learn to assert themselves or ruthlessly dominate others.

Yet, from the moment of birth, our behavior is completely caught up in a relationship with our primary caretakers — usually our parents. Getting their attention, getting our needs met for food, nurturing, adequate clothing and warmth is essential to our survival. Think how helpless a baby is. Then imagine what it must feel like to be a baby, alone in a crib. You're hungry, you cry. What if nobody comes? How does this make you feel?

Or your mother feeds you, but perhaps she's cold and distant and doesn't rock you and sing lullabies to you. She places you back in your crib once your bottle is empty, leaves the room, shutting the door behind her. What do you feel like now?

You can see that, as very small children, a lot of us learned quite early that certain emotions, behaviors or reactions were not acceptable or downright dangerous to display around our primary caretakers — and therefore, the world. Perhaps an alcoholic father didn't like being wakened by a colicky baby and became physically abusive. Perhaps a young mother with too many children to care for, sank into a depression and neglected her baby. Already as infants, we learned that being hungry for food or affection will drive a parent away; that being sick invites pain and fear.

When a baby cannot elicit a needed response from his primary caretakers, something happens to him. He learns to disguise or disown his true needs, his real self. As that child grows up, he becomes ever more disassociated from his true self. His sense of worth is based on things outside him. There is less internal happiness because there is little inner life.

Just after children are born they go through three important developmental stages that act as building blocks to a healthy personality and good self-esteem.

1. *Trust.* Infants need to know they can count on someone outside themselves who will act in a predictable manner, who will respond to their needs. When security and trust are present, a bond begins to develop between the child and the primary caretaker, exchanging positive emotions, such as: trust, love, delight, playfulness, caring and commitment. Since a child's world is so circumscribed, the only way he can develop a sense of self-worth is through another. What we see in our parents' eyes tells us who we are: how good, how lovable, how pleasing.

2. *Reciprocity.* Trust leads to a sense of reciprocity between a child and his parents. Reciprocity is like a bridge of shared experiences that connects the caretakers on one side with the infant on the other. The bond of trust allows the child to feel safe as he begins to explore the world. The bridge of reciprocal emotions that travel from parent to child and back again, is strengthened by certain experiences we come to expect and depend on. The child learns to rely on his parents' love, respect and caretaking.

3. *Autonomy.* At about the age of 15 months, the motor abilities that coordinate walking begin to develop and a child starts exploring his sense of autonomy from his

parents. You've seen toddlers start to let go of tabletops and wobble for a few steps on their own. They're experimenting with what it feels like to "hold on" or "let go" of Mommy or Daddy. As soon as they're able, they're off and running, roaming and exploring their expanding world. Exploring means touching, tasting and testing the boundaries — at all times. The more adventuresome the child, the greater his sense of autonomy. And a healthy sense of autonomy can only be developed if trust and reciprocity have been validated.

If the bond of trust, or the bridge of reciprocity is not strong, a child may cling to a parent, afraid to explore, or seem listless and distracted, unable to respond.

Of course negative patterns can occur at any time in one's development, but children are extremely vulnerable in early infancy, when many patterns — both good and bad — become solidly imprinted.

You may have already explored the nature of your early relationship with your parents or primary caretakers. For many, it is difficult to understand how we were treated as children or understand the feelings we coded in our self image because we lacked objectivity then. Yet, the kinds of feelings we stored about ourselves surface later in life. Adult self-esteem is frequently a reflection of how we incorporated our early experiences of trust, reciprocity and autonomy.

Ask yourself the following questions:

1. *Do I feel self-conscious when I try to express myself?* The drive to express our innermost selves — the part that hasn't changed since childhood that honestly registers and reflects our most heartfelt emotions may be stifled. If we learned as children that certain emotions were not acceptable, self expression may not be easy. It may even feel threatening.

2. *Do I have trouble confronting people when I think they've acted wrongly toward me or anyone else?* Children can be angry, especially during their "terrible twos", when they're pushing the boundaries of what they may and may not do.

At this age, children often react with screaming and temper tantrums. How your caretakers handled your anger is a key to adult confrontation skills. They may have been threatened by it, or felt it challenged their authority. If you have trouble confronting people you're angry with, ask yourself: Where does your anger usually go? Do you complain to others, or do you act it out in self-destructive patterns?

3. *Why can't I set goals and stick to them?* How many times have you vowed to start a daily weight loss regimen or exercise plan? Or to save more money? Most of us would like to be more disciplined, but if making a commitment to yourself is a real problem, it may indicate that during your childhood the sense of commitment was not developed.

Low self-esteem may indicate early abuse, either physical, emotional or verbal. When you goof up, do you immediately call yourself a name, "you stupid jerk."? Think back to when you were a child and see if you can recall how your parents dealt with your mistakes. By the way, it's part of being human to make mistakes. We're all here to learn, right? Did they call you "dumb" or "crazy" or yell "what's the matter with you, anyway?" Children pay close attention to what their caretakers think of them, no matter how bad it is. They often don't have the slightest idea that their parents are wrong, or that other adults think differently of them. Children can't recognize abuse until they have alternative adult behavior to compare the abusive behavior to.

4. *Why do I let people take advantage of me?* It's called "having boundaries and sticking to them." It's healthy to say no and have others listen. Perhaps when we said "no" in the past, we didn't sound like we meant it. If you don't enforce your boundaries, no one else will. Why else would your best friend call you at all times of the night, or forget to return the books you lent her? Why else would your children simply ignore you when you're disciplining them?

Having boundaries means we've defined who we are. "I'm a person who likes to be in bed by 10:30 at night," or "When I'm talking to you, I like you to acknowledge me," or "I don't do windows." Boundaries mean "no" to the rest of the world and we can expect a certain amount of friction as a result. If we're lax about enforcing these boundaries, it often means we weren't allowed to have them as children. Did your parents invade your room whenever they wanted? Did your parents respect your privacy and your right to make decisions without their interference? How soon after reaching the legal driving age were you permitted to drive the family car? When was the first time you said "no" to your parents? Did they listen? How did they react? How did it make you feel?

5. *Why do I keep getting in the same kinds of destructive relationships?* People always seem new and different at first, then it turns out I've chosen the same kind of person I always do.

The way we deal with the world is very similar to the way we dealt with Mom and Dad when we were children. Were your parents authoritarian figures, big on discipline and getting you to snap to? Some rebel at the first chance and may still be doing so at the slightest sign of an order. Authority figures may still be a problem for you, and now that you've got kids, you're supposed to be one!

Or maybe the folks were just too tough and you knuckled under, becoming Daddy's Little Girl, Mommy's Little Helper, or just an all around pal to your parents. You never got around to having a life of your own because you were too busy filling the gaps in theirs. Consequently, you became overly compliant, unable to display anger, rebellion, mouthiness — all those things that make being a teenager fun.

Even if, after vowing intensely to never fall for it again, you still find yourself choosing the same types: the overly-controlling egomaniac boyfriend, the manipulative, sexy girlfriend, the knight in shining armor who turns out to be a sourpuss, the best friend and roommate who rips you off and leaves town...maybe it's time to check out your primary caretakers.

Realize, too, that people change. It's likely that your relationship with your parents is quite different now than it was when you were an infant. But ask yourself some of these questions:

1. *Do I trust my parents to value me for the qualities I value in myself?*

   • Do they view your compassion and kindness as merely weakness?

   • Do they want you to be exactly like them? Are you?

2. *Did my parents encourage autonomy in their children or did they subconsciously encourage dependence?*

   • At what age did you get your first summer job? Whether it was by mowing lawns or babysitting, the money you earned was your first passport to financial autonomy from your parents. Were you encouraged to spend it or save it?

   • Did your parents show you how to balance your checkbook?

   • Were you ever allowed to take the bus downtown with a friend or were you always carefully supervised?

3. *Did your parents ever discourage you from doing things or having feelings because they were unacceptable for your age or gender?* Did they say things like:

   • "Girls don't become architects."?

   • "Boys don't take piano lessons. Sign up for football."?

   • "People your age don't go back to school."?

Most often, children with low self-esteem are the products of parents with similar problems. Those with high self-esteem, who truly love and accept themselves and others, know what a precious gift they have to pass along — to their children most of all.

EXERCISE NO. 2: EXPLORING EMOTION

Choose a color. Any color you like. Close your eyes and picture it. Is it flaming red-orange, fiery and hot-tempered? Is it a deep blue, calm and restful?

Now, be that color. Imagine you have become the color you chose. Write down all the qualities you ascribe to that color. Say what you do, what you are, how you make people feel. Be as forceful, as passionate, as intuitive or as brilliant as you want to be.

Now look at what you've written. How does that color mirror certain things about you? It can be very freeing to "project" our inner feelings into something as abstract as color. Try doing this exercise daily. Do your color choices change? Observe how you feel before doing the exercise and after. How do your emotions change? Write down your responses in your notebook.

SUMMARY

Being critical and judgmental of others is a sign of poor self-esteem. So is being overly demanding of ourselves in the form of perfectionism and workaholism, both classic low self-esteem syndromes.

The key to our poor opinions of ourselves can often be found in the past. How our parents treated us when we were infants and children set the pattern for the types of relationships we would develop as adults.

From the moment of birth, children go through three basic phases in forming a relationship with a primary caretaker.

1. *Trust.* Infants need to know they can count on someone outside themselves to act in a predicable manner.

2. *Reciprocity.* The bond between parent and child is strengthened by reciprocal emotions and shared experiences children come to expect and rely on.

3. *Autonomy.* The toddler begins to experiment with finding the balance between holding on and letting go. Parents need to let the child know they're there without interfering with the child's need to explore and test the outer world.

If not resolved or overcome, early negative patterns established between ourselves and our parents can continue to be mirrored in the relationships we form once we're adults. Were you allowed to:

1. *Express yourself?*

2. *Confront your parents when you were angry with them?*

3. *Learn commitment to your own goals and objectives?*

4. *Have boundaries?*

If problems from the past aren't examined, we're likely to repeat choosing the same sort of relationships over and over, by modeling the same kind of negative patterning that was imprinted on us as children.

3

MAKING A CHANGE
FOR THE BETTER

We've all heard about the power of positive thinking. Maybe you even tried "looking on the bright side" for a while and discovered that your world didn't change as quickly as your attitude. You still had bills to pay, problem bosses to deal with or complaining kids to shuttle off to school.

"This is real," you told yourself, "This is the way things actually happen. My work is unappreciated. My best ideas are stolen by bad bosses or co-workers. After all the time and energy I devote to my family and friends, they just want more. All that positive thinking stuff is just a stupid mind game." Then you grimly threw the positive thinking book into the trash, and settled down into being a full-fledged curmudgeon.

Well, guess what. You were right. Despite your positive attiude the world is unrewarding and crummy. Your window on reality is only a reflection of how you see yourself. Adjusting your attitude without working on your self-esteem is simply a quick fix that can only take you a short way down the track before a major breakdown occurs. As far as winning the race goes, you'll need a much more solidly-built vehicle to finish in the winner's circle.

So let's start from scratch.

You Are What You Think

Has something like this ever happened to you? You're used to dealing with the guy in the next cubicle like he's a computer nerd. Ron is nice enough, but kind of odd. You joke about him to your friends at lunch. You're pleasant, but not too pleasant when you see him coming down the hall — just enough to maintain a good working relationship. He seems shy and withdrawn.

Then one night you hear Ron on the radio. He's the guest on a talk show and it turns out he's one of the world's leading experts on African agronomy. Not only is he well-informed, but people on the panel address him respectfully, even humbly. They want to know what Ron thinks. They listen to what he has to say as he lucidly explains complex problems and encourages feedback. You can hardly believe your ears. He graciously thanks the host for having him on the show, telling the listening audience he will be lecturing at the local university next week if anyone is interested in knowing more about African agronomy.

You're stunned. Suddenly your whole concept of Ron turns upside down. The next day at work you don't know how to approach him. You say, "Hey, heard you on the radio last night. You were really good." He thanks you in his customarily abashed manner. But a look passes between you. Your relationship has changed forever. Now he knows that you know that he's not a nerd. Now you think of Ron as, just possibly, a great guy. Suddenly he becomes multi-dimensional, not just a one-dimensional joke. Oddly enough, when your respect for Ron increased, you felt better, too. As if you restored some of your own humanity by recognizing Ron's.

Or maybe this one fits.

You're not exactly the world's most adored father. Because your job demands that you travel a great deal, your relationship with your son falls somewhere between that of a screaming tyrant and an autistic TV viewer. Things are often strained and stressful when you come home. Sometimes you think your son actually dislikes you. He's often disrespectful and rude. Pushed to your limit, you become irritable and bullying. You're not proud of the kind of parent you've become.

Then you're asked to coach his little league team. Baseball is one of your favorite sports and you give it all you've got, molding the team from a bunch of undisciplined crybabies to a nucleus of decent players. They make it to the playoffs and finally win the league series. At the end of the last game you look into the stands and see a lot of parents grinning from ear to ear. After the excitement dies down and you're packing cleats and uniforms into the car, your son takes your hand and looks at you like you're a hero. In that moment, he's proud to be your kid. You look in the mirror that night and see a happy, contented father smiling back.

Even if you don't recognize yourself in these scenarios, you've had the experience of looking at yourself — or someone else — in a new light. A series of unforeseen events can make us temporarily lose track of how we're feeling about ourselves. And then what happens? Something momentarily blocks that negative feedback, and you feel good. You like yourself. It feels like your world is brighter, shinier — full of possibilities — not the least of which is you. Imagine what it would be like to be like this all the time. Well you can; that experience is the core of positive thinking.

How You Define Yourself

Take out your notebook and quickly write down ten things that describe you. Do this exercise quickly without taking time to think it through.

Now look at your list. What did you write?

If you feel like you're a good parent, for instance, did you list that? Maybe you feel inwardly like you're a poet, an undeveloped musician or a good caretaker of others. Perhaps you pride yourself on your gardening abilities, or your love of history, or your daredevil spelunking expeditions.

Chances are you wrote down some negative things, too. Perhaps you don't feel you make enough money, that you lack good looks or a solid education. Something may be standing in the way of self-acceptance. If you examine your list objectively, what's the little voice saying? "I'm not good enough?"

The reason we think we're not good enough is often due to the arsenal of guilt, criticism, fear and resentment we were armed with as children to keep the world at bay. Out of the hundreds of messages 2-year-olds hear from their parents in a single day, something like 32 are positive and 432 are negative. Parents often feel that the most expedient way to ensure a child's safety is by limiting his boundaries. Therefore, we grew up hearing messages like, "Don't touch that," "don't cross the street," "little girls don't wrestle," "it's not safe to climb trees."

Depending on our gender, we were molded to fit into slots society had designated as proper roles. Little girls were often taught to be compliant, quiet, self-sacrificing and not to hurt others' feelings. Little boys were encouraged to never show fear or pain — it wasn't manly to cry or be afraid. Consequently, we learned at a very early age that certain emotions were simply inappropriate.

The Four Evil Fairies of Our Childhood

Sleeping Beauty was attended at birth by three good fairies who heaped blessings upon her. Yet one evil fairy slipped into her cradle and condemned her to everlasting sleep once she was pricked with a magical spindle.

Most children love and idolize their parents. Even children of abusive parents would rather remain with their families than leave them. Throughout our childhood we looked upon our parents as the good fairies who were sent to protect and guide us at our most vulnerable age. Yet by instilling guilt and fear and by passing on their critical, resentful patterns, our parents often unwittingly played the role of the evil fairies as well. These negative controls on the part of our parents were to ensure correct behavior, yet they set up within us a belief that we lacked worth.

1. *Guilt.* If we heard messages about how "bad" we were as children, we tried to act in ways to earn our parents' love and acceptance. Consequently, children who experienced a great deal of guilt were brought up to please others, and deny their own needs. These children often became very sad, depressed adults. Worse, guilt-ridden adults often act out their guilt and need for punishment — by being in chronic pain and sometimes by committing crimes. The pattern of guilt is a dangerous one to maintain as an adult.

   Ask yourself how you feel when you do something simply to please yourself? Vaguely uncomfortable? Is it easy for you to be spontaneous, or do your feel nervous, as if you need someone's permission?   Can you give yourself praise, like "I needed to do that. That was fun. I'm really a good person." Or do you need to hear it from others? Some health studies suggest that children who were brought up with a lot of guilt messages often experience sore throats, tonsillitis and thyroid problems, for our larynx is where our voice originates — the instrument by which we proclaim to others who we are.

2. *Fear.* A fearful family environment is possibly the most damaging thing to children. They naturally want to explore, experience, ask questions and probe the world around them. If we're made to feel life isn't safe, it's difficult for us to live it fully and happily. As adults, our fears may translate into ulcers and back problems.

Fearful adults often disguise their emotions by exaggerated bullying behavior. When confronted with a child's emotion that triggers their own fearful response, they belittle the child, calling him names rather than offering support and understanding.

Fear is a powerful emotion with far-reaching consequences. It can envelop whole communities, even nations, during times of war or economic upheaval. A natural reaction to fear is to find a scapegoat, someone to blame. Narrow-minded religious communities often label ethnic groups or non-conforming individuals as enemies to be overcome, resisted, ignored or run out of town. Survival in such a community hinges on conforming and obeying the unspoken rules, not acting "different" or attracting undue attention.

Consequently, fear can squelch an individual's creativity and willingness to love. Overcoming fear begins by learning to love and value yourself.

3. *Criticism.* We have all been criticized by our parents and know that nothing produces such an overwhelming sense of unworthiness. Remarks like, "you never do anything right," "practice until you get it right," "you look terrible," "why can't you understand this simple math problem?" cause our self confidence to plummet like a stone. Critical parents were often criticized themselves. Their remarks may be produced by their own internal tapes about their unworthiness. Nevertheless, criticism is devastating. It's something we have little defense against. After all, if we had performed better, these people would not be criticizing us, right? There's no way to escape our own ineptitude.

Feeling critical of ourselves produces procrastination and self-loathing. Why should we be in such a hurry to get to where we want to go? We'll only find out how unworthy we are once we get there.

As we grow up, we shrink from critical remarks by teachers, bosses, spouses — even our own children. Worse, when under stress, we hear the same words coming out of our mouths directed at our own children. How can we stop the flow of critical abuse that filters down from one generation to the next?

One way to let go of criticism is to accept ourselves as we are, here and now. Release the habit of criticism and your self-esteem will begin to spring back to life.

4. *Resentment.* When we're resentful of others' success, happiness or material wealth, it means we have lost sight of our own goals and aspirations. We all possess different gifts, abilities and innate talents. Utilizing those abilities

is a matter of how much we're in tune with ourselves. Resenting others' good fortune is a barrier to our own growth and change. Held onto for a long time, resentment has been suggested as a cause of cancer and tumors.

Perhaps we were raised by parents who resented their children's ability to feel joy spontaneously, to participate freely with friends. They might have resented how much they sacrificed for us, how we were nothing but barriers in their lives, prefacing remarks with, "If it weren't for you. . . ."

When we find resentment clouding our relationships, we need to let go of the past and all the injustices it contains. Begin affirming your own uniqueness with statements like, "I am my own person and claim my unique place in the universe."

Starting Here, Starting Now

So how do you begin to build your self-esteem? Simple. Consciously begin to love yourself. Starting right here and right now. There will never be a more perfect moment.

Think of yourself as a Christopher Columbus, about to undertake an exciting new voyage of self-discovery. You'll be able to weather any stormy sea that threatens your self-esteem as long as you know a few basic laws about universal self-love.

1. *What we think about ourselves becomes the truth.* It's not what others say about us, it's what we say about ourselves that matters. If you think you're unworthy, you'll never feel good about yourself, no matter how many outer trappings of success you acquire.

Conversely, if you love yourself, others will find you lovable. Your self concept accepts whatever you choose to believe and selects experiences to mirror that belief. This is an important and powerful concept to understand. Your self concept acts like a dutiful genie, unthinkingly carrying out the orders you give it. If you say to yourself, "I'm such a mess. I don't deserve to be happy. . . to win this race. . . to share my life with such a great person. . ." your subconscious mind takes this as a blueprint for the future and builds on it.

When we've been raised with lots of negative messages — such as criticizing ourselves, or never taking risks because we're fearful of the outcome — it's difficult to grasp how deeply our subconscious mind has been imprinted with these patterns.

> 2. *We create our experiences by our thoughts and feelings.* Our underlying thoughts and feelings are conveyed by how we express ourselves in words and actions. If you find yourself saying predominantly negative things, you can change this verbal pattern. It indicates a subconscious negative attitude toward ourselves. Daily affirmations are an easy weapon you can use to combat negative thinking.

Affirmations are simple statements you repeat that reprogram your subconscious mind. They are ways to "remind yourself" of what's important — who you are, what your goals are, what patterns you are working on changing. One powerful affirmation for building self-esteem is the simple exercise we did at the end of Chapter 1, saying, "I love and accept myself exactly as I am." You may want to do affirmations for material success, such as, "I am open to material prosperity from unlimited sources."

We'll discuss affirmations in depth in the following chapter, but realize that your future begins now — at this very moment. If you always thought that "some day" you would get it all together — when you were more financially secure, when you were thinner, when your children were grown, realize that the only time you have control over is this very second. The building blocks of the future can be found in the thoughts and words you're speaking this very minute. To have a future filled with security, purpose, love and fulfillment, begin shaping it today.

> 3. *What we give out we get back.* Do you think of the world as a scary place, filled with people "out to get you" or is it a challenging, life-enhancing environment, filled with people willing to help and even to love? Whatever your definition of "what's out there," that's what you'll get. Reality has an odd way of confirming our expectations.

Against his friends' advice, one professor of sociology at a Midwestern college went on a 5,000-mile solo bicycle trip in 1987 without a dime in his pocket. His mission was to prove that there is goodness and genius in everybody. He felt that being dependent on those he met for food and shelter would help break down barriers. He asked people along the way for help and found it in the form of beds, breakfasts, grilled cheese sandwiches, hot showers and plenty of friendly chats. After contacting more than 500 people on the road, the professor encountered only five who refused him help.

Examine some of your belief systems and see how your views of the world become self-fulfilling prophecies — for good or bad.

4. *Make a break with the past.* No matter how deeply you've been wounded by others or what rotten decisions you've made that have hurt others, it's important to let go of old emotions. Resentment and a desire for revenge can prevent us from achieving happiness, by trapping us in meaningless patterns of negativity. It is just as useless to go on punishing yourself for things you might have done differently. Realize the past is over and done. You cannot change it. It's time to get on with your life.

Remember, the best thing about the present is that it is the door to opportunity. Like a snake shedding its skin, you may be ready to release your old self and grow into a new, more powerful, more positive person. You may already be fantasizing about the kind of person you're going to become, but seizing the opportunity today is your point of departure. You can realize this by affirming, "My life is in a state of renewal. Each moment of my life is new and fresh and vital. This is a new day. I am a new me."

When we're contemplating a change, there is a tendency to negate everything we ever were. "I made such a stupid mistake by getting married too young," you tell yourself, or "I'd never spend money as foolishly as I did two years ago." Remember, people with high self-esteem incorporate and never negate what they were or the decisions they made. The past is a powerful tool if used in the right way. It contains the answers to accepting the true you. As painful as it may be, take a long, loving look at the changes you've been through since childhood and embrace and accept each one. Try the following exercise to get in touch with the part of you that was an infant. Don't worry about being absolutely sure that the feelings that surface were there when you were a baby. It's okay to let your imagination go and fantasize.

EXERCISE NO. 3: IN THE BEGINNING

Using one of the photographs of yourself as an infant, close your eyes and hold the picture close to your heart. Breathe deeply, concentrating on how it must have felt to be a baby. Imagine how new and strange and exciting the world looked to you then. Feel your mother holding you in her arms and rocking you to sleep. Now look into this child's eyes and realize there is only one thing this baby wants from the adult you — unconditional love.

Visualize holding yourself as a baby in your own arms. Tell the baby how much you love and care. Admire everything about this perfect child. Say that it's alright to make mistakes, you're there to understand and protect this child within you.

Keep the photograph where you can see it often and repeat the exercise. What kind of feelings surface? You may feel a "bonding" between this early part of you and the adult you now are. As the child within starts to get some needs met, how does your behavior change? Are you less critical of others? Does your appetite for food decrease? Is it easier to breathe?

Learning to love yourself is a powerful way to dissolve negativity.

SUMMARY

Building your self-esteem involves more than just an attitude adjustment. Your self-esteem is regulated by your subconscious mind which, like a giant movie projector, beams your own self-image back at you from the screen.

Our ideas about ourselves and others are pretty deeply in-grained. Think about the last time your self-esteem got an unexpected boost from another person's opinion of you. How did it feel to be a hero for a day? We often define ourselves through negative statements and images which can be leftover childhood patterns. The four most common negative patterns are:

- Guilt.

- Fear.

- Criticism.

- Resentment.

You can change the way you feel by changing the way you look at the world. It's important to seize upon and act within the present moment. We have total control over our futures once we realize that:

1. What we think about ourselves becomes the truth.

2. We create our experiences by our thoughts and feelings.

3. What we give out, we get back.

4. We can make a break with the past.

Above all, don't reject any part of yourself or any experience from the past. Finding the true you depends on loving yourself, starting with the helpless infant you were, and incorporating feelings all the way through the awkward teen and reckless young adult years. Look at all the snapshots of yourself in the family album — even those garish ones when you wore fadish clothes! Affirm that you love and accept yourself through all your changes. Learn to recognize and honor the child within.

4

TAKING THE
POSITIVE APPROACH

Bad attitudes, like bad colds, are catching. Have you ever noticed that when you're in a really rotten mood people either avoid you or become just as irritable and grouchy themselves? So much of our personal success depends on how the world sees us. When we appear strongly motivated and positive, others want to be around us and bask in the reflected glow of our self-confidence. When our self-esteem is low, it's easy to draw others into the vortex of our negativity. Maybe we have a reason to feel defeated, cynical and cheated, but there's a way to deal with life's setbacks so that they don't poison our outlook and destroy our self-confidence.

Think of the road to success as a smooth, straight surface, paved with high self-esteem. You value yourself, you have clear boundaries, therefore, others value you — even when they disagree with your opinion. You have defined your goals and you're making headway. You know there will be obstacles, pitfalls and difficult patches to be negotiated, yet you have what it takes to get there — belief in yourself and a positive attitude.

When your self-esteem is low, it's as if you've taken a detour off the main road and gotten lost in a maze of confusing, circuitous back roads. A negative attitude keeps you focused on small, unpleasant annoyances rather than the big picture. You complain about all you've endured: the series of flat tires, broken water pumps and empty gas tanks. Your traveling companions agree — you certainly have had a run of bad luck. Silently, they wish they had gone in someone else's car. You wander around in circles, growing ever more dissatisfied with your plight. Destinations and goals no longer exist. Occasionally, you wonder how you strayed so far from your original purpose, but most of your effort is spent in struggling with the stretch of road just ahead.

Live the Life You Choose

If, as a child, the only time you received any attention was when you were sick or hurting, then you might subconsciously place yourself in situations as an adult in which you're perpetually victimized. We are all free to choose.

And just as we are free to choose, we are free to change. The present is the only time in which we can do so. This is the good news. The bad news is that when we look at the situations we love to complain about. . . that we never get to do what we want, we can't please anyone, we lack talent, nobody cares about us. . . we must partly look to our own behavior.

So what's holding us back from making these sweeping changes for the better, from leading more complete, fulfilling lives? One answer is your subconscious mind — that industrious little genie that whispers self-defeating messages in your ear, that erodes what confidence you may have developed and, in general, helps you realize your worst fears about yourself.

Think about how you describe your life. Do you say, "I am

happy and content. I have all I need," or do you complain and grumble, "I can't do anything right. My life is completely wasted. Everything's so boring." Whatever your subconscious hears, it remembers. Then it goes to work making it come true.

Consider, too, that your words merely reflect the deep-seated thought patterns that govern each waking moment. No wonder there may be a huge conflict between our conscious wishes, "I want financial stability," and our subconscious beliefs, "I'm totally undeserving of anything good. I'm bad."

So, how can the marvelous freedom to choose ever reprogram the dutiful genie that thinks it's working for a bad, lazy, morally reprehensible boss? The answer lies in words and pictures. Visualize and verbalize consciously and you'll change the structure of your subconscious. Instead of living a life that continually frustrates and baffles you with its setbacks and limitations, you'll be living the life you choose to live. Here are some ways to do it.

Affirmations

What we think about ourselves becomes the truth for us. What we want for ourselves becomes what's possible for us. It's proven that the more you expect from situations, the more you'll achieve. Maybe you don't feel comfortable taking a strongly positive approach. The world of limitations is more familiar to you. At least you know what the perimeters are, what you can and can't do.

You're shy, for instance, and avoid parties and gatherings where there are lots of people. You're used to saying, "I'm just not good in groups of people. I'm too sensitive. I'm better one-on-one." This may be true, but lately a promotion at work demands that you be more outgoing. Besides, you're tired of being a wallflower, of hearing second-hand, all the gossip that makes parties fun.

We all admire people who can walk into a room confidently and start chatting with anyone they meet. How about that guy at the wedding reception who, with no prompting from anybody, started singing "Volare" at the top of his lungs? And remember that polished woman at the last cocktail party who came all by herself and mixed so easily?

One way to overcome something in yourself you want to change is to affirm the change. Affirmations are simple statements, usually short, declarative sentences that proclaim a fact in no uncertain terms. If, for instance, you'd like to feel more confident at social gatherings, say, "I like people and they like me." Repeat this sentence several times a day before the big event. Practice it at work, practice it at home. Say it just before you drift off to sleep at night and when you wake up in the morning. Repeat it as you take those deep breaths before stepping into the room filled with party guests. Then watch what happens. The more you have repeated the affirmation, the more powerful its effect on your subconscious. People may actually like you better because they sense you're more relaxed and confident. As they gather around you, your self-esteem soars and you realize you like them. Parties are fun, people are great!

You might even try varying the affirmation to fit your expanding social network: "I like a wide variety of people and they like me." Or, "I attract good friends who like and respect me," or, simply, "I love and am lovable."

Here are some simple rules to follow about creating the right affirmations for yourself:

• Affirmations are clear and brief.

You get confused with an elaborate affirmation like, "I am writing a book that I want the agent in New York I haven't met yet to really love." Define what you're trying to do: attract a good agent for your work, right? Put this desire into a simple statement, "My book attracts the right agent."

• Affirmations need to be strong and positive.

Using the party example, the affirmation to help you overcome shyness is a powerful one, "I like people and they like me." You set up a flow of energy between the positive message you're sending out to others ("I like you!") and the positive message you're getting back ("We like you!"). If instead, you had said, "I hope that others will like me at this next party" that introduces the possibility of doubt and failure to your subconscious.

Many researchers believe affirmations that contain negatives don't work because the subconscious hears only the positive statement. If you're trying to stop smoking, for instance, don't affirm, "I am no longer craving nicotine," for your subconscious hears, "I am craving nicotine." A better affirmation might be, "I am free of nicotine."

- Affirmations take place in the here and now.

By affirming a condition in the present, it becomes your reality. See how powerful this statement is, "My job provides me with financial abundance now" compared to "Next year I'll get that promotion to increase my income."

It may seem irrational to affirm financial abundance when you only have three dollars in the bank, or to affirm your physical health when you've just come down with the flu. But rather than confirming negative patterns that support self-doubt and fear, you can choose affirmations that effectively counteract your present situation. They serve to jolt our subconscious into another reality based on self-esteem.

- Affirmations grow more effective with repetition.

The first time you say an affirmation it may sound strange, exotic, even slightly boastful or silly. You may feel vaguely embarrassed saying, "My talent is perceived and well received by all who. . . (read my book) (see me dance) (hear me speak) (watch me act) (stroll through my garden)." You'll find, however, that while writing your book, or learning the lines of your play, the affirmation quiets your fears and starts to build your self-esteem. You even start to enjoy visualizing the looks of surprise and delight on your audiences' faces. As you plant a new bed of brightly mixed daylilies, imagine how visitors to your garden will drink in the flowers' beauty. Slowly, the affirmation becomes woven into your daily reality. Nothing is more gratifying than to reach an end of a project . . . taking curtain calls, autographing your new book. . . and realize this moment from real life was contained in the kernel of your affirmation.

Why Affirmations Work

Affirmations work because they give our subconscious mind permission to start making long-needed changes. We need to shake up old concepts that no longer work for us. Maybe you don't know exactly how you want to change, you only feel restless and dissatisfied. Try this affirmation, "I am willing to change and release old negative beliefs." You may not realize what old beliefs you're ready to give up, but announcing your willingness to do so opens up channels for creativity within your subconscious.

Affirmations can be said any time during the day, but they're most effective if repeated in the morning as we wake and in the evening as we drift off to sleep. Said in the morning, an affirmation acts as a motivator for you to concentrate on your overall goal: "I am a creative and dynamic person." Said at night, affirmations can reprogram our subconscious and reinforce self-esteem as you sleep. "I love and am lovable."

It's good to write your affirmations and keep them where you can see them. One successful writer has covered his study with affirmations that motivate him: "I am writing a best-selling novel," "my work is well-written and well-received." Or, "writing is easy and fun for me" (which it often isn't!). Other people travel with affirmations on sticky-notes stuck to their dashboards: "I receive good from unexpected sources of the universe."

Visualization

All of us have negative people or things in our lives we'd like to change or get rid of: a critical mother-in-law, a dead-end job, a house that's always a mess, a to-do list of things that never get done. Instead of concentrating on the negatives, it's important to release the pattern in us that created these conditions.

Our imagination is one of the most powerful tools we can use to create change. Our subconscious mind dutifully constructs our reality from the pictures we give it. You can use visualization to your advantage either as a separate exercise or in conjunction with your affirmations. If your affirmation is, "I like people and they like me," imagine yourself being surrounded by a circle of happy, enthusiastic friends eager to share with you.

As Emmett Fox, one of the pioneers of positive thinking, wrote, "The secret of successful living is to build up the mental equivalent of what you want; and to get rid of the mental equivalent of what you do not want."

At the end of the day, sit quietly in a comfortable chair. Concentrate on your breathing and gradually regulate your rate of respiration. Notice how your heartbeat slows down. Feel all the day's anxieties and cares floating away from you. Now, very quietly, begin imagining the ideal you. Are you more slim and fit? Are you wealthier, living in a grand style? How do you occupy your time? With work that absorbs and fulfills you? By exploring a hidden talent? By helping others? Do you hold a long-awaited newborn baby in your arms? Are you opening the mail and finding a check for your first screenplay? Perhaps you have found spiritual peace and contentment. Or maybe you live in a snug, cozy cabin in the mountains and spend your days raising bees, collecting honey and enjoying the spectacular natural scenery that surrounds you.

Obviously, our ideal day holds endless possibilities. Sift through all the elements and find the ones that feel right for you. Don't worry about how "doable" any of these ideal pictures are. This imaginative energy is also called daydreaming, only visualization can be channeled, directed and controlled.

Perhaps there's a part of you that always wanted to be an actress. Begin picturing in minute detail how you will look, where you will receive your training, what kind of plays you'll appear in, what sort of celebrity you'll become. Don't hold back. What will your country house look like? Your town house in London? Who will come to your parties? Will you get an Oscar? The more detail you add, the stronger your visualization becomes.

Or perhaps you always intended to get into shape, but now it's practically too late. Visualize yourself jogging each day. Is this enough or does it lead somewhere else? Do you see yourself entering the Boston marathon or a triathalon competition? Let your imagination go. Take yourself to the pinnacle of success in everything you visualize.

How Visualization Works

When we clearly visualize what we want on a regular basis, we are showing our subconscious a definite plan of action it can follow to make our dreams come true.

You can make visualization work for you by following these simple guidelines:

1. *Relax and breathe.* Find someplace in your house where you can be comfortable and have privacy. Create whatever kind of environment feels right for meditation and relaxation. Light a candle if you like, or burn incense. You can play soft, soothing music — whatever creates an atmosphere of peace and tranquility. Now begin regulating your breathing. As you inhale more deeply, visualize yourself going within — to the most personal, private part of you. Imagine yourself going deeper like a deep-sea diver until you're submerged into your own essence. Whatever is not you — daily worries, trivial concerns, emotional burdens — drift away into the atmosphere. You are in touch with the most fundamental part of yourself.

2. *Allow yourself to feel what you need.* Like a child feeling its way along a darkened corridor, let your feelings, not your thought processes, guide you. Begin to feel what it is you most deeply want and care about. Is it to be more nurturing? Is it to unleash your creative abilities? Is it to protect the world's delicate environment? Go with whatever feels right for you. Don't worry about whether it makes "sense" or is in keeping with your present lifestyle. Pay attention to how "good" it feels — how fulfilled this new concept makes you feel.

3. *Visualize in detail.* Like a new homeowner furnishing a house, start fleshing out the details of your visualized fantasy. Perhaps you want to write a book that will help people and be an enormous success. Don't worry about the book's details. Those problems are for your conscious mind to resolve. See your book being read by millions of people who are grateful to have the information you've given them. Visualize the thousands of letters that will

deluge your mailbox and the pleasure you'll receive from reading them. See yourself at book signings, on talk shows, responding to the success your book has generated.

Whatever your fantasy goal, make it real by making it detailed. Cut out pictures of role models or goals that are objects (like your "dream house") from magazines. Perhaps you're thinking about buying a log cabin in the Rockies, or you admire the movies Steven Spielberg makes. Look for pictures of cabins or film directors to "flick the switch" of your subconscious. When you find a picture that enhances your visualization, tear it out and pin it up on a bulletin board where you can see it. You might want to keep the pictures in a special "dream album" so that when it comes time to build your home, remodel your kitchen or plan a summer vacation, you have a wealth of ideas to choose from. Visual images can help your goals take shape quickly.

5. *Make visualization a regular part of your life.* The more time you spend visualizing your goal, the more real it will become. When you start to spend time on a regular basis visualizing your goals, they become a familiar place where you can recharge and relax. Daily updates and detailing helps keep you in the present. Visualization should be connected to your most deeply felt heart's desire. Keep your visualization rooted in your true desire, and stay relaxed about it. Don't get rigid or overly-controlling about your visualization. Let it flow and develop naturally.

Visualization can be a powerful means of physical and spiritual healing. Cancer patients are frequently taught positive self-imaging as part of their therapy in overcoming the deadly disease.

One of the most important aspects of getting affirmations and visualizations to work for you is the ability to let go, no matter how chaotic or unsatisfying your life seems. Proclaiming this affirmation in the midst of a stressful situation allows you to stop worrying, let go and allow more positive energy to flow through you that can create changes for the better.

Still doubtful that visualization can have a major impact on your life and self-esteem? Then look at it this way. Think of the powerful effect negative, self-defeating mental images have already had on your life. Haven't they become a reality to one degree or another? In the past, your mental images may have been negative, but now is the chance to substitute positive images. You have nothing to lose and everything to gain.

EXERCISE NO. 4: SEEING IS BELIEVING

Visualize a goal that is important to you. It can be something short-range, like better day care for your children, or long-range, like a better job, new house, etc. Focus on it mentally so that you can write it down in a simple sentence: "Our family is enjoying the space and beauty of our new home."

To make more of an impact on your subconscious, it helps if you can find a picture of the kind of house you want. It should be one that is affordable, yet meets your needs. When you find the ideal picture, cut it out and paste it on a piece of cardboard. Use it in your daily visualization. If it's not colorful enough, add some additional details with magic markers. Cut out photos of yourself and your family and place them in and around the house. This technique is called "treasure mapping" — making the ideal real by using your imagination and power to visualize.

Now write an affirmation that goes with the picture. "My family has never been so happy as in our new home. It is everything we always wanted. We can afford it, it gives us privacy, beauty and peace."

Now sit quietly and visualize your family and you in your new home. See it in all its exquisite detail — including the kinds of shrubs and flower beds you'll plant, how you'll decorate the childrens' rooms, the comfortable, spacious living room, the functional kitchen.

Keep your ideal scene in a notebook, by your bed, or hanging on the wall in the room where you do your meditations. Read your affirmation often. Keep a log of any changes you make to your visualization. Record the time it takes for the visualization to become real — noting the date of your initial imaging and affirmations and final moving day.

SUMMARY

Your attitude can change for the better when you fully realize that rather than being life's victim, you are living the life you choose to live — whether it was consciously or subconsciously mapped out.

Once we realize we are free to choose, we are free to change. The only time we can make these changes is in the present. The words you choose to describe your daily life reflect the thought processes that govern each waking moment. Negative underlying concepts can sabotage all your best intentions.

You can change subconscious patterning through pictures and words: by positive visualization and affirmations.

Affirmations:

1. Should be clear and brief, strong and positive.

2. Take place in the here and now.

3. Are more effective with repetition.

Our imagination is one of the most powerful tools we have to create change. Visualization works because:

1. By utilizing relaxation and guided imagery it employs our imagination to provide our subconscious with new blueprints for our future.

2. It can become an integral part of our daily lives.

3. It builds upon detail. The more sensory your visualization, the more real it is — and the more quickly it manifests itself in reality.

5

GOAL-SETTING

Nothing makes your self-esteem soar like achieving a goal you set for yourself. Conversely, nothing can be more disheartening than failing to meet a goal. When our self-esteem is low, we refrain from setting goals, telling ourselves, "why bother, I'll never do it. It's just too [boring]. . . [difficult]. . . [time-consuming]." What we're really saying is that we are afraid to confront the possibility of failure.

But without clear goals, it's too easy to drift through life, making no definite commitments to ourselves. We may wake up one day and find our children grown, our days pretty much our own and yet we still haven't found the time for those golf lessons we wanted to take when we turned 30.

Why Goal-Setting Builds Self-Esteem

Perhaps the trickiest part of getting what we want out of life is deciding what it is we want. This is where goal-setting can help. One major misconception about goal-setting is that you must know exactly what you want before you set goals. Actually, one of the best ways to clarify what you want is to set goals. While achieving them, you can constantly re-evaluate whether or not your chosen path is the one you want to pursue.

Have you ever noticed that when you set a goal — a new car, a more challenging job, a vacation in Australia — it manifests more quickly? That's because you're more focused, more in tune with your daily actions. Your subconscious makes sure it's leading you straight to the perceived goal.

When goal-setting works properly it raises your self-esteem because it:

1. Challenges you to overcome patterns of failure or limitation.

2. Allows you to be more tolerant of failure in other areas of your daily life.

3. Gives you confidence to set increasingly adventuresome goals, to explore areas you've neglected.

4. Makes you see life as part of a process. Achieving a goal won't make your life perfect, but it will improve it.

5. Allows you to get on with your personal development. An achieved goal can bring new awareness of what you ultimately want.

Goal-Setting Traps to Avoid

One of the reasons we don't set goals is that the process can cause a certain amount of anxiety about getting measurable results. Since goals are dreams with deadlines, they can connect the here and now with the process of achievement. If we're not used to goal setting, planning, organizing and reviewing can make us very uncomfortable.

After setting a goal for yourself, monitor your behavior. You may find yourself acting out various avoidance techniques: overeating, oversleeping or watching a lot of TV. You may even become depressed or overwhelmed. If these feelings arise, allow yourself to experience them. Monitor your reactions, but continue the goal-achieving process. Keep a daily log of those emotional reactions. You might be surprised when you read it later. You'll find things like "felt like I was coming down with the flu today, but ran three miles anyway. Didn't do as badly as I thought I would. Now I feel fine." Your resistance reactions can be precious clues as to the ways you avoid getting what you want in life.

There are, nevertheless, some traps associated with goal-setting. See if any of these sound familiar.

1. *Overly-complex goals.* The initial goal-setting process is an exhilarating one. It's fun to think that in just one month, we'll be 50 pounds thinner, have a new car and have written the perfect marketing plan at work. Don't allow yourself to get carried away with goals that are too complex or unachievable. You'll feel overwhelmed, confused and discouraged, and your self-esteem will take a hit.

2. *Goals that aren't measurable.* Maybe you want to be a better parent, spend more time with your children and be happier while you're doing it. How do you know when you've achieved this goal? After you take your kids to the latest movie? After you bring them breakfast in bed on Sunday? After you let them have their friends sleep over on Friday night? The never-ending challenge of "being a better parent" will exhaust you with overwork and your guilt won't magically go away.

Instead, spend some time thinking about what would mean a lot to you and your children. It should involve a measurable amount of time with a definite deadline: say, a camping trip. Get your kids in on the planning stage so they can share in the excitement. If it's something you've never done before, set up a goal that actually translates into everyone having more fun together.

3. *Goals that aren't what you want, but what you think you should want.* Here's your chance to leave preachy old Mom on the front porch while you roar off in the shiny red convertible you always wanted. Don't get caught up in setting goals that are "sensible" or "mature" or even logical. You may be spending the next year of your life in achieving this goal, so make it fun, experimental. If we set goals for ourselves that are too safe, conservative or limited in concept, our desire to achieve, like a bored child, goes to sleep. If, on the other hand, we're planning a walking tour of England, a raft trip down the Colorado River or taking our first glimpse of outer space through Mount Palomar's telescope, we're undoubtedly going to get more enthusiasm.

Goal-setting is for ourselves alone, not something we do to please others.

4. *Being overly rigid about goals.* When they're properly conceived, goals are based on feelings that can be described as "touchstones." For instance, you may have a goal of becoming a lawyer, but this is actually based on the touchstone of using your intelligence as an advocate for the defenseless. You decide after your first year of law school that it isn't really what you had hoped, but you stick with it because your goal was to become a lawyer. After your second year, you've had enough, and end up working with the homeless in job training.

Although your goals changed, your touchstone, "helping the defenseless," didn't. The feeling behind your original goal remained on track. Your means of expressing it merely changed form.

5. *When we don't meet goals — how to deal with failure.* Although the possibility of failure is inherent in everything we do, its results for most of us are too crushing to contemplate very long. No one wants to fail — especially at meeting a personal goal you're committed to. However, there's a lot to be learned from failure. It's like a signpost saying, "this goal wasn't appropriate for you. Look over here instead."

Some of the world's greatest success stories have been built on failure. In a recent study of four millionaires who had set themselves goals to have $1 million by the age of 35, each had held, on an average, 18 jobs before striking it rich. They learned from failure what didn't work for them and quickly redirected their energies.

Everyone learns from failure. For instance, you might find that what you thought you wanted — a cabin in the Ozarks — simply wasn't for you. Although the cabin never materialized, you realized spectacular scenery wasn't enough. You became bored and restless in the rustic Midwest. What you really wanted was a condominium in San Francisco. And so you adjusted your sights and redefined your goal. Understanding that failure is not a judgment about our inherent abilities, intelligence or personality is a true sign of healthy self-esteem. Failure is simply part of the process of finding out where we want to go.

If you have failed to meet a goal, deal with it consciously. Don't push it to the back of your brain. Ask yourself if it is a goal you want to set again or whether you want to let it go. It's important to acknowledge unmet goals this way, otherwise they stack up in your subconscious under the heading of "failures" and create resistance to further goal-setting.

How to Set Goals Effectively

Goal-setting is the key that unlocks the door to positive self-esteem. It should be fun and exciting. The thought of making changes, though, is always a little bit scary. You may want to set up a group of like-minded friends who are ready to make changes in their lives. Or you may feel more comfortable working on your own. Just remember, however, that when you hit a snag — and you will — groups are an effective way to get you past the rough spots. When you've worked as a group from the beginning, other members can keep you energized and focused. How you choose to work is up to you.

Here are some important steps that will make your goal-setting sessions really do the job.

Giving Up the Past

Remember how great it felt last spring when you finally got around to cleaning out your closets? You had put it off for a number of years, actually. You were amazed at the clothes you hauled out of the forgotten dark recesses. Some you had outgrown, some were hopelessly out of style, some you had been hanging on to for sentimental reasons. Those Betty Grable tap shoes, you finally admitted, just might look better on someone else. And then you had the garage sale and nearly all the stuff sold. The rest you trucked down to the nearest Goodwill store.

Remember how it felt to walk into your house and see those clean, empty closets, no longer bursting with wrinkled, squashed, unattended clothes? It felt great. You started to breathe easier. It felt like starting over.

Goal-setting is a form of starting over, but it requires a kind of spring cleaning before you begin. It's called "clearing."

You need to clear out psychological blocks that are holding you back from attaining your goals. You can find out where these are by paying attention to your body. Notice where you feel the greatest amount of constriction, where tension blocks the flow of energy through your body. Take a few minutes and breathe deeply. See where you feel "tight." Is it in your chest, your arms, your head, your stomach?

Blocks are sometimes caused by repressed emotions of fear, guilt, anger and resentment. These unacknowledged negative emotions can cause you to tighten up and close down spiritually, mentally and emotionally.

To get yourself moving, you must explore the area in which negative emotions are stored and reconnect the old emotions in a positive, loving way. Negative emotions are a good chance to examine negative belief systems that need discarding, just like outgrown clothes. For clearing to work, you must learn to do two rather dissimilar things simultaneously.

1. Love and accept yourself compassionately for having this belief.

2. See clearly that you're ready to let go of it, because it's limiting, self-destructive and untrue.

For instance, you might have been raised with an alcoholic parent. As a child, you learned that to display your true emotions invited an unpleasant, even violent, response. You had to shut down emotionally and deny certain feelings and emotions.

Now that you're an adult, it's still difficult for you to open up to others — particularly to partners. Most likely, you're storing a lot of anger, grief and resentment against the parent whose love you so badly needed and never received.

Take a deep breath and see if the area around your heart seems constricted. The heart can represent the center of love and security for many. As a child, you might have closed off any kind of loving give-and-take, and in so doing, cut off the joyful expression of life. Now your daily life reflects strain and stress, not joyful acceptance. Try saying this affirmation and see if you feel the difference: "I lovingly allow joy to flow through my mind and body."

Or perhaps you stored your fear of criticism in your stomach — if so, you might have chronic digestive problems, such as colitis, ulcers and abdominal cramps. These problems may represent a fear of life and the need to stop its process. Perhaps your parents were overexacting and critical, doling out love sparingly and only when certain conditions were met.

Repeat these affirmations, or revise them to fit your needs:

"I love and approve of myself. I create my own joy. I choose to be a winner in life."

"I trust the process of life. I am safe."

"I am at peace. I am calm. All is well."

As you move into the areas where you feel the greatest tension, it helps to write down the negative beliefs that come to mind. Sit quietly in a comfortable chair with paper and pencil in your lap. At the top of the paper, write, "The reason I can't have what I want is..." Breathe deeply and visualize that you're sending that breath highly charged with love and compassion and energy into the area where you feel blocked. Now write down the negative beliefs that come to mind. How do you feel? Don't resist feeling anger, sadness, fear. When these feelings arise, realize they are simply "waves" of emotion, and that you're floating peacefully on top of them. Breathe into them, experience them deeply, then release them. Your list may look something like this:

"I can't have what I want because...

- I'm too lazy.
- I'm bad.
- My spouse wouldn't like it.
- It's too hard.
- I tried it once and it didn't work."

Now look at your list. In doing the breathing exercise you might remember when you acquired these negative beliefs. Maybe you began thinking you were lazy after that summer you stayed with your fussy Aunt Mildred, or it was that terrible fourth grade teacher who kept telling you that the next reading level was too hard for you. When you feel you've finally gotten in touch with your negative beliefs, tear up the paper and either throw it away or burn it. You want this part of your life to be over!

Now sit quietly and release the past by doing some affirmations to replace your constricting, limiting beliefs. You might want to say:

"I now release my entire past completely. I am free!"

"I now dissolve negative, limiting beliefs. They have no power over me!"

"I don't have to try to please others. I am naturally lovable and likeable no matter what I do."

Forgiveness

Nothing keeps us so totally wrapped up in past problems as unexpressed feelings of anger, resentment and desire for revenge. How many times have you had someone tell you about a childhood enemy or a college roommate with whom they're still upset? The anger erupts as violently as if the event happened yesterday, and yet it was years, sometimes decades, ago. Forgiveness is the key to letting go of the past and its power over us. Forgiveness allows us to get on with our life.

Write on a piece of paper the names of all the people who have ever harmed or mistreated you or dealt with you unjustly. It can be anyone you feel hurt, anger or resentment toward. Write what they did to you and why you feel resentment toward them.

Now close your eyes and visualize that person clearly. Explain to them why you have felt hurt and angry with them in the past, but add that you're going to do your best to forgive them. You wish to dissolve the constricted energy between you. Repeat: "I forgive you and release you. Go your own way and be happy."

Write at the bottom of your piece of paper, "I now forgive and release you all," then throw the paper away or burn it.

Most people experience a miraculous lightening of their spirit after they do this exercise. To make the clearing exercise complete, repeat it, only substituting a list of people you feel you have harmed or treated unjustly in the past. Close your eyes and imagine each person in turn. Tell each of them what you did and ask them to forgive you and give you their blessing. Imagine them doing so unconditionally. Write on your piece of paper, "I forgive myself and absolve myself of all guilt, here, now and forever." Then tear up the paper and throw it away.

You may want to accompany this spiritual and emotional clearing with an actual physical clearing, such as cleaning out those closets and drawers, inflating the tires on your bike or getting your sewing machine fixed. You're setting your "house" in order — on every level. It helps to accompany this activity with clearing affirmations:

> "The more old, negative feelings I release, the more space I create for good things to come to me."

> "I am now putting my life in order, preparing to accept all the good that is coming to me now."

Brainstorming

Now you're ready to start setting some goals. You may have a lot of ideas bouncing around in your head, but no real feel for a specific, targeted goal.

1. *Defining Goals.* It may not seem like buying a new couch for your living room could have a great impact on your goals for work, but any goal you choose will somehow affect every part of your life. Saving the money to buy a new couch, for instance, could determine how aggressively you go after a promotion at work. It's important to realize that although our lives are compartmentalized into different areas, they are subtly woven together into a single fabric. One type of goal (a more appropriate career choice) could be enhanced by meeting another type of goal (singing lessons for self-expression).

Make a list of these six categories:

1. Work and career.

2. Lifestyle.

3. Relationships.

4. Creative self-expression.

5. Travel and leisure.

6. Personal development/education.

Without thinking too deeply about them, write down quickly under each category some things you would like to change in your life. Perhaps you feel that your present relationships with friends and family are okay, but you'd like to expand your horizons a little. You'd also like to take some evening classes at the local university and would consider going for a master's degree in Anthropology.

Travel and leisure, you think, sounds like an advertisement for an exotic cruise aimed at the rich and famous. But write down something anyway — say, spending leisure time more productively, not stuck in front of the TV — maybe visiting a few local museums.

Now look at what you've written down. Prioritize which goals seem to be more important than others, but don't toss out any of them. Perhaps you're horribly bored at work and want to move on, but lack the training or education to do so. You've decided, however, to enroll in the master's program in Anthropology and that seems very exciting. Maybe your goal list looks something like this.

Work and career: Find a new career eventually, don't know what. Only have B.A. in Anthropology.

Lifestyle: Buy new car sometime within the next year. Relationships: Family stuff okay. Volunteer for voter registration drive. Need more stimulating friends.

Creative
self-expression: Could be much better, but what? Singing lessons?

Travel and leisure: Take kids on a canoe trip this fall. Or a vacation to the Grand Canyon after buying the new car.

Personal
development/
education: Enrolled in master's program in Anthropology. Will take classes on part-time basis for next three years.

Prioritizing

Rank your goals in order of importance. As you prioritize which ones you want to work on immediately, you'll see that some are short-term goals, accomplished in a fairly simple manner and some are long-term goals, requiring a great deal of planning, reprioritizing and networking.

To decide what's of utmost importance to you, do the "energy test." If you know someone who's engaged in the same goal-setting process, or even have a good friend willing to listen (and suspend judgment), have them make a tape recording of you describing your goals. Afterwards, when you play the tape, listen to where you put the most energy. You'll hear the tempo of your speaking pattern speed up, grow warm with enthusiasm and glow with confidence when you start talking about the goal that means the most to you. Is it taking the canoe trip with the kids or is it getting that master's degree in Anthropology? Wherever you have the greatest level of enthusiasm, that is what you should make your number one goal.

Remember, there is no value attached to your favorite goals being long-term or short-term, intellectual or creative, fun or hard work. You might already be working 10-hour days at work and the thought of re-entering academia is too draining. Or you might need that canoeing weekend for yourself alone, leaving the kids. Just listen to yourself objectively on the tape. Which goals do you daydream about, see endless possibilities for?

The "Touchstone" Behind the Goal

Let's say getting a degree is your favorite; that means making all your other goals of secondary importance to your primary goal. Now, define the "touchstone" behind the idea of getting a master's in Anthropology. What does it consist of? Perhaps you think an M.A. in Anthropology will get you a better job. This is information you need to check out. How many M.A.s are working outside of academia and how many are enrolled in Ph.D. programs?

The "touchstone," remember, is the feeling behind the goal. A master's degree in Anthropology promises you three years of interesting classes, taking in new information, discussions with professors, doing research, writing papers and some field work. Boiled down, it translates to "intellectual stimulation with a limited chance for meaningful employment when it is completed."

By meeting your primary goal, you also have the chance of fulfilling your secondary goals: You could meet stimulating people; you might even travel a bit and there's a chance that, by doing outstanding research, your creative self-expression would be enhanced. Your lifestyle and work/career goals would definitely take a back seat until the program was completed. Examine how you feel about putting those on hold. How important are they to you?

Short-term and long-term goals

There's another drawback to having a highly structured, exhaustive, long-term goal. Yes, if you complete it, you'll feel immensely better. But do you have a chance of getting there? Be honest with yourself. Look at your life situation. Are you married with children or single? If you're single, you can make changes more easily than if you are responsible for children. Once committed to a project, do you feel trapped, growing impatient for change, or are you willing to slog it out, and reap the eventual rewards?

Every person is different. There's nothing wrong with deciding halfway through a master's program that it's too much work, it will take too long, and you've had enough of these stuffy academic types. Goal-setting is most effective when goals can be accomplished within a reasonable period of time. That's where establishing short-term goals can be helpful.

Look at your touchstone again. What is the feeling achieving the goal will awaken? Meaningful work with intellectual stimulus, right? Look at your options with just a B.A. in Anthropology. They may not seem overwhelming. But there might be a way to satisfy the touchstone behind your goal without going through three more years of school. This is where you may want to take a look at other resources (see below). Once you know where you're going, the idea is to get where you want as quickly as possible.

Whatever you decide, long-term goals, such as finding meaningful employment, cannot be achieved without setting short-term, achievable monthly or even weekly goals. Think of them as stepping stones you lay down daily that lead eventually to that far-off goal on the horizon. Short-term goals need to be updated constantly. It's good if you can have someone to report to on a monthly, or even weekly, basis. Long-term goals can represent deeply-desired fantasies and needs for sweeping changes. Even these goals, however, should have deadlines attached. Five years is the usual allotment of time given in which to meet long-term goals.

It helps to write down your five-year goals in the form of affirmations, as if they had already been achieved. You can work for a stronger, clearer picture of what you want.

"I now do important field research on South American tribes.

My work keeps their forests and traditions from disappearing."

Now write down your one-year goals. Make sure they support your five-year goals, that they're all flowing in the same direction so that when you accomplish your one-year goals you will be one step closer to reaching your five-year goals. They might look something like this:

"I am completing my first year of work as an Anthropology graduate student with straight A's. A professor has recommended me for a grant next year that includes travel to South America."

Now, write out your goals for six months from now, one month and one week from now. Keep it simple and choose the three or four that are most important. Be realistic about how much you can accomplish in a month (take the GRE exam), or a week (write application letters to various universities). Accompany these with affirmations, such as, "I am reaching my goal step-by-step, day-by-day." "Scoring well on tests is easy and fun for me."

Resources

Working in a group increases the flow of energy much more dynamically than working alone. You will find, as you work toward achieving your goals, that getting where you want to go is never simply the result of determination and single-mindedness on your part, although staying focused is critical.

Have you ever heard famous people talk about how they got where they were going? Great success stories usually contain some particle of starving in garrets, paying one's dues and honing talent through rough times. But eventually someone loaned the celeb-in-the-making a helping hand and offered him his first lucky break. That's what people are for. Look at friends, family and even complete strangers as your greatest resources. It's called networking.

You can rely upon others for a number of things:

- *As mentors.* If you know someone personally who got where you want to go and is successful at it, ask them if you can "interview" them and have them advise you. Believe it or not, most successful people are dying to talk about how they made it and will be happy to share "how-to's" with you. They might even go a step further and critique your manuscript, put you in touch with their agent or encourage you to take a class they're teaching. Find out what they need from you. All networking needs to include reciprocity.

- *As heroes.* Who are your heroes? Alexander the Great? Abraham Lincoln? George Sand? Anna Pavlova? Jane Goodall? You may choose heroes for their accomplishments, their bravery, their talents or their kind hearts. Pin up their pictures on a bulletin board or the wall by your desk where they can inspire you daily. Be prepared to be disillusioned. Our heroes all too often have feet of clay. Abraham Lincoln suffered from severe depression, Anna Pavlova was an egomaniac. You can overlook their weaknesses though, and focus on what makes them appropriate role models for you.

- *As conduits to sources of information.* Perhaps you need to know what kind of crops grew in your area during Neolithic times, or you'd like to look through a telescope just once and have someone explain why it works the way it does. Or maybe you just want to ask that author one short question about Adlai Stevenson's political career. You may not have direct access to this kind of information, but depending on the size of the group you work within, or the number of people you know, almost everyone knows someone who can help you. It may not be quite in the way you envisioned, but networking works. The more vast your array of business associates, friends and fellow members in professional groups, the more rewards you reap. Effective networking is how you can find a great job with only a B.A. in Anthropology — through people who already know you, like you and respect your work.

- *When giving is better than receiving.* Groups also ensure that your talents are being tapped by helping others. If you have ever worked in a volunteer capacity, you might have noticed a curious dynamic. Eventually, giving to the group becomes more important than what you get out of the group. This can only occur in an altruistic atmosphere where members have learned to trust one another and selfish motives are left at the door. The effect is inspirational and there can be no greater boost to one's self-esteem than to know you have actually helped others in a very tangible way.

The following exercise is geared to make you think about the reasons behind goal-setting. Time is one of our most precious, finite resources. How well we use it determines whether or not we meet our goals. But what if time was not a consideration? Sound like a luxury? It is. Go ahead and enjoy it in this exercise.

EXERCISE NO 5: GETTING THERE.

One of the toughest parts of goal-setting is figuring out what part of your incredibly rich and diverse nature you want to explore.

In this exercise you're going to be able to be all the things you ever wanted to be without having to give up any of them. Imagine that you have five lives to lead. What would you do with each one? If you can't fit everything into five lives, then make it ten. If you can't think of enough to fill up five lives, then make it three. You can go backwards and forwards in time. For instance, maybe you always wanted to be a tragic cabaret singer like Edith Piaf, as well as a great scientist like Darwin and why not an amateur 19th century balloonist?

Don't worry about your "lives" fitting together. They're all valid, important parts of you. They're what make you your lovable self. Okay, have a go. Write down the five lives you would most like to pursue and go into as much detail as you want. Do these ideal lives mirror any aspect of your actual life? How do they affect your goal-setting decisions? Do they help you re-prioritize what's important?

SUMMARY

Goal-setting boosts self-esteem because, if done correctly, it can get us where we want to go. Without clear goals, it's too easy to drift through life, never making a commitment to what we truly value. You don't have to know what you want to achieve before you set goals. Often the process of goal-setting will make that clear. Effective goal-planning does take some practice. Traps to avoid are:

1. Overly-complex goals.

2. Non-measurable, undefined goals.

3. Goals that don't reflect your true desires.

4. Being overly-rigid about goals once they're defined.

5. Not realizing the benefits of failing to meet a goal — what failure offers is a chance to redefine and re-prioritize.

Some preliminary steps help us to set goals more effectively. Clearing, for instance, relies upon getting rid of past patterns, including eliminating physical blocks to the flow of energy within your body. These physical blocks, or areas of tension, are "holding areas" for psychological blockages often caused by unresolved anger, fear and resentment.

Clearing is facilitated by forgiving those who have wronged us and whom we have wronged. Truly forgiving and releasing old enemies from our consciousness helps get new, creative energies flowing.

Brainstorming, either alone or with others, is a great way to define goals for various aspects of our lives. Once they're objectively listed, we can prioritize them in order of importance.

Remember that specific goals may change, but the "touchstone" or feeling behind the goal remains the same. Evaluate your goals and determine which are short-term and which are long-term. Arrange the short-term goals so they help accomplish the long-term goals.

While long-term goals should reflect our innermost fantasies, our highest ideals or most exalted visions, we should be able to accomplish them within a specific deadline. One way to short-cut endless cul-de-sacs in getting to our goals is to make use of the human resources within our circle of friends and acquaintances. After you have stated clearly what you want, networking is one of the most effective ways to work through others to achieve goals.

6

SELF-ESTEEM AND THE FAMILY

Some say charity begins at home. So does self-esteem. How we learn to value our uniqueness largely depends on how well our parents managed to convey their love and appreciation of us. In previous chapters we examined the early imprinting we received as children and how those messages affected our self-esteem. Now it's time to look at how we, as adults, nurture self-esteem in other family members, be they partners, children, siblings or even aging parents.

The Family as a Movie

We've all seen movies about families, whether they're the creative screwballs in "You Can't Take it With You," the tragic perfectionists in "Ordinary People" or the heartwarming couple in "It's a Wonderful Life."

Look at your own family as you would a group of characters in a movie. There may be the harassed mom, the sports-obsessed dad, the rotten teenager, the tattle-tale kid sister. Think about the roles people in your family have played, beginning with your mother and father and extending to your own children. Does your rebellious daughter remind you of your judgmental mother? Does your husband remind you of your father when he's being particularly aloof? Are people always telling you how much you act like Grandma — an old lady in a lavender dress you can barely remember? And how do those roles change as people age? Your parents were probably more lenient with their third child than with their first. And just look at that bratty brother of yours who ended up teaching art in elementary school.

Sometimes roles get assigned to us — even before we are born. Fond relatives may tell us they always knew we would turn out to be a handful, we were such active babies! We may not like the roles we're given but we're almost powerless to change those roles as long as we're in the grip of the family. To advocate change is to go against the flow that was established early in each family's history about who the successful ones would be, who the failures would be, who is smart, who is dumb — even who is attractive and who is not.

Sometimes the only way to change roles is to change movies —that's why so many people literally blossom once they leave home. Even when they have received plenty of nurturing and love at home, teenagers yearn for the personal growth that comes with discarding outgrown roles.

Using Your Family History to Your Advantage

No one wants to completely reject their families, even when we've been "typecast" in roles we really don't enjoy playing. Maybe our parents labeled us as the under-achieving black sheep, or the shy middle child, but out in the "real" world we found we could overcome those limiting concepts.

Yet when holidays roll around and we're together for the ritual Thanksgiving turkey, all sense of time disappears and our self-esteem slowly begins to erode. To our own horror, we actually do start acting like the bashful child we once were or the teenager with an attitude.

Next time try this experiment. It is guaranteed to not only boost *your* self-esteem, but everyone else's as well. Do a little digging in your family archives and find out all you can about some of your ancestors. Maybe your mom's grandparents were Norwegian immigrants. Ask your mom and her sisters to get out the old photos and tell you everything they can remember about their forbears. How did they learn English? Did they go through immigration at Ellis Island? How did they save enough money to buy that land in Wisconsin? Interview aunts and uncles, encourage them to talk about the "old days"— the depression, the War (I or II), the first house they bought in the suburbs on a G.I. loan. You'll learn a lot. Grandparents, especially, can be living history books.

Unearthing your family's history is a fun way to learn about all the fascinating people you're descended from — the rugged pioneers, the visionary businessmen, the healers and nurturers who held the family together during crises. Life was not always as comfortable or secure as it is now. You'll appreciate your parents more and understand the societal forces that shaped them.

Most important, you'll start appreciating yourself more as you hear stories that sound remarkably like your own. As your dad tells you about your Great Aunt Alice and what a terrific piano player she was, you'll finally understand where your musical ability comes from.

Your parents too will benefit from your interest. Dusting off the family album gives them a chance to step outside their defined family roles. Once your dad sees that picture of himself in 1942 before he shipped out to fight in Germany, he'll be flooded with recollections, good and bad, but nevertheless memories important to his self-esteem.

For people who like to remain in tight control, taking time out to reminisce can be emotionally threatening. If parents want to cling to a particular unexamined reality, then let them. But by reviewing the past — no matter how painful — we are able to see life as a continuum, as a series of options and choices that we made. Even when it seems we made the wrong choice, there was always a lesson learned, a deepening of our character, a challenge met.

Self-Esteem in Partnerships

When our family consists of just two adults, roles can often be a little looser because the adults aren't also caretakers. Or are they?

We have all seen relationships that seem like a remake of "Whatever Happened to Baby Jane?" The husband seems pretty normal and his wife acts like a fossilized child — whining, pouting, hanging all over her husband during dinner. In short, demanding his attention and approval at all times. We wonder how the poor guy can stand it. Or how about the reverse, where the smart, professional woman is married to a guy who insists on treating her like a child — acting insanely jealous if she decides what to order from the menu without his supervision.

Although they're extreme examples, such relationships do exist. They're created by people with low self-esteem who seem destined to a lifetime of abuse — whether it's physical or emotional. Statistics show that women whose husbands physically abuse them were often abused by their fathers. As a species, humans seem to like patterns, good or bad. Low self-esteem dictates that we seek demeaning situations and stay there — no matter how much we have to manipulate others or lie to ourselves to do so.

On the other hand, healthy relationships based on high self-esteem allow partners to experience a great deal of personal freedom while expressing their love for one another. Emotions are not manipulated, cajoled, forced or repressed, but allowed to flow more freely. Roles aren't assigned based on traditions, sexual stereotypes or neurotic patterning, but on perceived needs and methods of meeting them.

Traditionally, relationships have exacted a higher price on women's self-esteem than men's. Until they began to enter the work force in the late 1950s, women were viewed as the primary caretakers of others — including their mates. Recent studies have shown that the average woman will spend 17 years caring for her children and 18 years caring for her aging parents. Not much time for self-expression. Obviously, most of the old expectations still linger. See if any of them fit you:

1. *Are you tempted to solve everyone else's problems at the expense of your own needs?* You've asked your mate to do the dishes every other night, but he begins to sulk. Do you give in to his emotional pressure and wash the dishes, or do you say, "You've got a problem. Deal with it."

2. *When men complain, women try to fix the problem.* When you complain, how does your mate react? Does he tell you to stop whining? See if fixing his problem is based on your fear of losing the relationship you're dependent upon. You may be holding on to it — no matter what the price.

3. *Do you feel it's a woman's place to "make everyone happy?"* Change necessarily brings discomfort and imbalance. Is making an important change too threatening? You want to take an evening ceramics class and you need the family car, also you won't be home to fix dinner. When your mate responds negatively, do you continue the class or drop it?

4. *Can you strike the balance between feeling empathy for others' feelings and self-interest?* It is possible to acknowledge the other person's feelings without becoming a compulsive caretaker. To do this, you need to figure out your priorities. If you're studying for an exam, and your mate is still sulking over the dishes, can you acknowledge his feelings and say, "You look unhappy" without rushing in to do the dishes?

Another telltale sign of a healthy relationship is one in which both partners are free to flaunt their individuality. Perhaps you really like to sculpt in metal and your husband likes to cook, or you think show tunes are the greatest, while your husband prefers riding his ten-speed across Iowa. No sweat. They're all winning combinations. Where creativity is concerned, there are no do's and don'ts. There are no rules, except to do what you really enjoy.

That's why it's so scary. Some relationships are based entirely on rules — about what's appropriate for men and what's appropriate for women; about what I get to do if you get to do this. There are even rules about how... (whatever it is you want to do)... will affect the children, the neighbors, your job. Eventually, the price for self-expression becomes so high, partners just stop paying it.

Respect is another earmark of a solid relationship. People with high self-esteem have a healthy respect for themselves. They identify with people they respect — especially marriage partners. Two people who respect themselves and each other are like a pair of powerful horses who can pull each other through life's quagmires and cross the finish line a winning team.

Building Self-Esteem in Your Children

You think you're doing pretty well with your kids. You're an open, understanding parent. Then one day, you're pushed to the brink. You've had a bad day at work, you ask your 10-year-old to clean up his room and two hours later, nothing's been done. You find him lying on his bed, his headphones on, listening to some demented, howling band.

"What's the matter with you?" you scream, "Don't you ever listen to what I say? You're lazy and selfish. Turn that tape off this minute and get moving."

He looks up at you, incredibly hurt, and slowly removes the headphones. With an overwhelming sense of guilt you realize you just replayed one of your tapes — one from your own childhood in which your parents screamed at you, called you names and compared you to the household's most non-productive relative.

You try to make amends and apologize, "Look, honey, I'm sorry. I'm exhausted. I had a really terrible day at work." But it's not enough. Your son mumbles that it's okay, but you know it's not. You both go away feeling miserable.

The relationship we have with our children is probably the most important one in our lives because we're actually responsible for shaping a human being's social reactions from the moment of birth. Children are so dependent upon their parents as caretakers that it's difficult at times not to feel overwhelmed. You want to do a good job of providing for them physically, emotionally and culturally. You want to make sure they study hard in school, learn to respect others, are self-sufficient, find out what they're good at and — somewhere along the way — have fun.

For all these things to happen, you only have to concentrate on one objective: building your child's self-esteem. A child's world can be a very scary one if they don't feel good about themselves. Since they have few experiences to compare their reality against, home becomes their universe. If the parents are overly-critical, blaming, judgmental or quick to punish, the child has little recourse but to internalize the concept that he is "bad."

Children are almost preconditioned to internalize guilt. When their parents are divorcing, for instance, the child usually feels it's his fault. Even children of physically abusive parents feel somehow to blame. A child's world is a voyage through an uncharted sea of emotions in which parents, teachers and occasionally adult friends are the only reliable guides.

Therefore, the single greatest legacy you can give your child is the gift of self-esteem. How you treat your child will largely govern how he treats his own children. Think of esteem building as setting a pattern your child will pass on to his children and on through the generations. In equipping him with self-respect and self-acceptance, you might even be breaking the pattern of centuries of negative conditioning.

Here's how to start:

1. *Accept, don't deny feelings.* This goes for you as well as your child, but since parents can often act as the guardians of their children's feelings, you need to be sensitive about how you react.

We deny our children's feelings for a number of reasons. Sometimes it's because we know they're feeling pain, embarrassment or confusion. To help them out of this uncomfortable place, we offer a glib explanation. When a child comes to us and says, "Mom, my teacher yelled at me today and everybody started laughing," our most common response is to say, "I'm sure they weren't laughing at you, Tim." The truth of the matter is, maybe they were laughing at your kid. That's what kids do. So by denying your child his interpretation of the incident, we add confusion to the embarrassment.

Sometimes we deny feelings to get children to stop behaving in a way we find annoying. You're on your way home after taking your son to the dentist and he's complaining about how much his tooth hurts from the filling. Rather than acknowledge his feelings, you say irritably, "Come on. Stop whining. It can't hurt that much. Why, I had four fillings once in one appointment and I never cried."

When children's feelings are brushed aside in such a manner, the child may become angry. He senses that his parents don't respect him, that his feelings are unimportant or that he's not being listened to. Try role-playing the above scenes, using the following skills.

- Actively listen, give your child your full attention.

- Resist the temptation to jump in and "fix" the complaint. Instead, reflect your child's feelings through questions or statements that indicate you heard what he said.

- Experience the empowerment that comes with being genuinely helpful.

When your child tells you about his day at school where everyone laughed at him, listen for the underlying feeling he is describing. It's probably embarrassment. Try responding by accepting, not denying his feeling:

"That must have been embarrassing, Tim."

It might feel weird at first not to shift the emotional burden from your child, but you'll be surprised at how eagerly he'll open up and continue giving you information. Eventually, through the dialogue, you'll come to a resolution.

"Yeah, but you know what, Mom? Yesterday we all laughed at Scott when his glasses broke."

"That sounds like it was embarrassing for Scott."

"Yeah. Laughing at people really isn't so cool."

Remember, the more you try to push a child's unhappy feelings away, the more he becomes stuck in them. The more comfortably you can accept the bad feelings, the easier it is for kids to let go of them.

2. *Avoid blaming and accusing, name-calling and threats.*
Nothing is more damaging to a child's fragile self-esteem
than to be called "stupid" or "a slob" or to be told that the
way he eats is "disgusting." It's only natural that parents
and children want different things from each situation.
Parents want a house they can come home to that is orderly
and quiet. Kids could care less. But these varying expectations create tensions that often erupt into wars with
authoritarian parents going after the rebel troops. Of
course, neither side ever wins these pitched battles, but the
emotional damage can be devastating. Why fight at all?

The purpose is to engage cooperation. You can't do everything it takes to run a house, help with homework, get yourself
ready for work and tend to your kids' daily crises all alone.
Besides, you want them to assume responsibility and learn how to
participate, being more able to share.

For instance, your 8-year-old begged you for a dog. You ex-
plained that the family could have a dog, as long as your daughter
would feed it and take it for a walk once a day. You come home
from work and find that the dog hasn't been out of the backyard and
is completely out of food and water. You explode at your daughter
who is watching TV, saying, "You don't deserve to have a pet! I
told you what the conditions were. You're too lazy to have a dog!"

You swore you wouldn't take an accusatory tone with your
daughter. And now the armies are mobilizing for a counterattack.
Take time out, change out of your work clothes, breathe deeply and
try this new approach:

- *Describe the situation.* Look out the window and say, "I
  see Brandy pacing up and down in front of the gate." Try
  to avoid adding manipulative phrases like, "sure looks
  like he wants to take a walk." Your kid will hear the
  underlying expectation and continue to resist. By
  describing the situation, you're giving your daughter the
  chance to take action on her own without submitting to
  your will. Who has the upper hand doesn't become the
  issue.

- *Give information.* When the dog's food and water dishes are empty, give information instead of fault-finding. It doesn't attach blame and jump-start the insidious guilt cycle. Instead of nagging, "How many times have I told you to be sure that Brandy has water on hot days?" say, "the dog's water dish is empty."

- *Talk about your feelings.* If your daughter's whining about having to take the dog for a walk is getting on your nerves, tell her, "Honey, I need to concentrate on getting dinner organized right now. I don't appreciate the whining. Besides, someone needs to take Brandy for a walk before it gets dark. Maybe you'd like to switch jobs. You can fix the green beans and I'll take the dog out."

When your children fail to cooperate on a simple household task, don't lecture or berate them. Rather tell them why it's important to you. "I don't like Brandy being neglected when we talked about the dog being your responsibility. Remember, we decided on this before we got Brandy."

Be willing to listen to their agenda, too. Maybe taking care of the dog on a daily basis is too much responsibility for your daughter. Take time to listen to her feelings. Maybe there's an underlying message. She's frightened that she'll lose control of the dog while he's on the leash; or that he'll chase another dog or bark at a neighbor. Keep the discussion open. Let her know your feelings, too. "Katie, I'd feel better if I knew that Brandy had been walked by 6 p.m. Lots of times we're busy in the evening, and I don't think it's fair for him to wait until 9 or 10 p.m. for his walk. What do you think?" Enlist your children's help in reprioritizing and problem-solving.

- *Show them the big picture.* "If we take Brandy for a walk now, that means dinner will be an hour late. Can you wait that long?" The process of adult decision-making often can be mysterious to children — sometimes adults deliberately obscure information or forego lengthy explanations to avoid arguments. But it helps for children to know about cause and effect. How, for instance, if they don't spend money now, they'll have more to spend on their summer vacation at Disney World. Or how, if they get in the habit of walking Brandy at a certain time, the dog will be calmer and better behaved.

3. *Invite them to be problem-solvers, not problem-causers.* When children cause problems by misbehaving, discipline can be either harsh, lenient or somewhere in between. Parents who are strict disciplinarians often bend their child's will to their own, allowing them little say in how problems are resolved. Children who were harshly disciplined by their parents can often become overly strict and inflexible themselves, adept at denying their own feelings and those of others. Complete leniency, on the other hand, is no solution. By misbehaving, children often push for guidelines. They want to know where the limits are. They want to know, if they challenge authority, does anyone really have it?

A child can easily feel threatened by a home in which there are no rules. How you deal with disciplining your child can give him valuable tools for self-correction once he becomes an adult.

For instance, if you're a working parent and your child doesn't come home immediately from school, panic often sets in. You feel powerless to rescue your child. You have had to phone parents in the neighborhood to locate your son and this naturally causes you distress. You've asked him hundreds of times to return immediately from school, phone you and tell you where he will be. Why can't he follow through on such simple actions?

- *Talk about your child's feelings and needs.* Show him you're interested in what he feels. You have respect for his needs, too. You can open the discussion by saying, "I know it probably isn't easy for you to leave your friends when you're playing Nintendo." This lets him know you're not presenting the situation from your viewpoint alone. It invites him to comment, to explain, to expand.

- *Talk about your feelings.* "But you know, I worry when you're late. I don't know where you are. I worry when I can't find you." (Avoid taking an authoritarian stance. "Young man, you'd better call me pronto at 3:30 each day or you're in world of trouble.") Let him see the situation through your eyes and understand your true concern.

- *Brainstorm a solution.* Ask him for input. Say, "Let's put our heads together and see if we can come up with some ideas that would be good for both of us." As he makes suggestions, write them down. When you're through brainstorming, take a look at your list and see what solutions you want to keep. "Let's see. If you're going to be playing at a friend's house, call me from there." Ask him to help you prioritize responsibilities. "But how about homework?" "Maybe I should do it in this order: come home, call Mom, get homework done first, then go play if I've finished my assignment." "That sounds good, Tim. Let's put this list up on the refrigerator so we won't forget it."

- *Reward kids for doing it right.* All too often the adult world seems fraught with so many rules and regulations that kids get exhausted trying to remember them all. When your child does actually do what you've asked him to, be sure to reward him positively, and not act like good behavior was simply expected. The reward can be as simple as a hug or the smile in your voice he hears over the phone. It can be something you like to do together, or his favorite treat. "Your grades were really good, Tim. This calls for bomb pops and then we'll rent one of those turtle movies." Conversely, children need to understand that not fulfilling the terms of an agreement has its consequences. Whether you discipline your child by taking away his freedom or having a serious discussion, he needs to know that laws of cause and effect actually exist, that parents have power to reward and punish and that he can choose between right and wrong behavior. Punishment should always be accompanied by an explanation of why you're taking such action.

- Give them a sense of autonomy. Children need to know they can function successfully outside the home. School is the first environment in which they usually do this. As they grow older, give them more responsibilities and allow them more freedom to move out into the world and explore. Give them information about how to take care of themselves, but teach them the world is a safe place.

By encouraging your 13-year-old daughter to take on baby-sitting jobs, you accomplish several goals: She develops a source of income and with it comes the decision to save or spend money; she has meaningful interaction with younger children, for whom she might act as a role model, an older sister, a friend; she learns how to solve problems independently; she sees how other families live. It's important for children to learn how other families are different from their own and how they're similar. It helps in developing the value systems they'll incorporate as adults.

Encourage your children to be productive members of groups: boy scouts, basketball teams, characters in the school play. Remember, that part of developing autonomy lies in the freedom to make what parents view as the "wrong" choices. Don't rush in to correct the mistakes you think your child is making. Allow your child to live with the consequences of his or her choices. Self-esteem doesn't come from always having done the "right thing." Some of the best decisions seem terribly wrong at the time we make them.

Self-esteem comes from meeting and triumphing over life's challenges. Realize that your child has his own unique path to follow. As he grows up, and becomes more autonomous, your role as advisor, helper and mentor needs to lessen in significance. We want only the best for our children. After holding on tightly to them as children, letting go lightly can be a challenge.

EXERCISE NO. 6: GETTING IN TOUCH WITH THE INNER CHILD.

Close your eyes and breathe deeply. See yourself as a child, maybe 5 or 6, playing around the house, then in the yard playing with your friends. See your parents when you were this age. Experience the feelings you had then. Did you feel love and acceptance from your parents or did they often fly off the handle, blaming and accusing you for everything that went wrong? Touch briefly on that center of pain within you caused by blaming yourself at such a vulnerable age.

Now realize that you are an adult. You can forgive your parents for the pain they caused you. Repeat whichever affirmations seem right for you: "I have all the love I need within my own heart." "I am whole in myself." "I am letting go of the old and making way for the new." "I now forgive and release everyone in my life. We are all happy and free." By forgiving and releasing your parents, you allow yourself to be a source of healing for your own children.

Now picture your actual child as clearly as you can. Ask him if there is anything he would like you to do for him, if there is anything in particular he needs from you. You may hear the words "I need your love, Daddy," or "I want you to spend more time with me." See all your child's problems dissolve. You might want to say an affirmation created especially for this child about how much you love him, value him, and will always be there for him.

SUMMARY

People get assigned roles in families just like they do in movies. If you feel "typecast" in a role you've outgrown or are no longer comfortable with, it's more difficult to change it than you might think.

There are various ways of circumventing your family's negative definitions and false expectations so you don't unconsciously play the role you were handed. One way of building your self-esteem within the family is by realizing there are no "good" or "bad" ways of being, there are simply preferences. Who's to say what is "good" and "bad" behavior as long as it doesn't prevent others from achieving their ultimate good?

Another esteem-building tactic is to research your family's history. There is always some nutty relative dangling from the family tree that everyone else wrote off as being "weird," "strange" or just plain "different." Get your family to talk about their past: their childhood on the farm, their young adulthood surviving the depression. It's a good way to discard institutionalized family roles — if only for an afternoon — and get a glimpse of your parents the way they were.

Building self-esteem in your children is an investment in the future. You'll be breaking the chain of inherited abuse — whether it's resentment, criticism, bullying, or fault-finding — that children have endured for centuries. You can build your child's self-esteem by following a few simple steps:

1. Accept, don't deny his feelings.

2. When disciplining your child, avoid blaming, accusing, name-calling and threats. The purpose is to engage cooperation, set limits and teach your child self-discipline, not breed resentment and rebellion. You can do this by describing the situation that needs attention; giving your child information about cause and effect; discussing your feelings honestly; and showing him the big picture of a process he may only partially be aware of.

3. Invite children to be problem-solvers not problem-causers by talking about their feelings and needs; talking about your feelings; and together brainstorming a solution.

4. A child's self-esteem grows in proportion to the amount of autonomy he experiences, first within, and then beyond the family. To prepare your child for successful functioning in the outside world, give him plenty of "how-to's"; encourage him to get an appropriate job (baby-sitting, lawn mowing) and control over his own money; support him as he makes his own decisions (right or wrong). Self-esteem comes from meeting and triumphing over life's challenges.

7

CONCLUSION

Building your self-esteem is the single most important thing you can ever do for yourself.

It's a common fallacy to believe that our lives will be improved once a certain event occurs, or once we acquire a long-coveted possession. But if we examine our desires closely, it's easy to see that attaining them will not bring true happiness, only momentary fulfillment. What has to change is within. Self-esteem is one of the major building blocks with which we can accomplish change and experience a greater sense of peace and security.

Although it seems elusive, self esteem begins when we honestly examine our emotions. How we feel towards others tells us a great deal about how we, as children, felt toward ourselves.

Negative habits such as judging and criticizing others can be overcome when we cease to judge and criticize ourselves.

Anyone who has ever tried to change an emotional pattern knows it's not easy. We have, however, two important tools in the form of affirmations and visualization. Seeing is believing. By repeatedly focusing on the positive, and giving your subconscious a new verbal and visual "blueprint" for the future, you'll see immediate results in an improved self-image.

The best thing about self-esteem is that it's available to everyone. No matter what kind of childhood you had, building your self-esteem will put you in touch with your own inner power. It's a deepening, strengthening process that enables you to make positive changes in your life.

Think of building your self-esteem as an investment in the future. Psychologically healthy adults have healthier children, less prone to self destructive behavior.

You can change your life by changing how you feel about life. When you're coming from a better place, the bad times are less threatening, and the good times are more frequent.

So what have you got to lose? Make that investment in yourself. It's one you'll never regret.

INDEX

Buy two, get one free!

Each of our handbook series (LIFESTYLE, COMMUNICATION, PRODUCTIVITY, and LEADERSHIP) was designed to give you the most comprehensive collection of hands-on desktop references related to a specific topic. These handbooks are a great value at the regular price of $12.95 ($14.95 in Canada); plus, at the unbeatable offer of buy two at the regular price and get one free, you can't find a better value in learning resources. **To order**, see the back of this page for the entire handbook selection.

1. Fill out and send the entire page by mail to:

   National Press Publications
   6901 West 63rd Street
   P.O. Box 2949
   Shawnee Mission, Kansas 66201-1349

2. Or **FAX 1-913-432-0824**

3. Or call toll-free **1-800-258-7248** (**1-800-685-4142** in Canada)

Fill out completely:

Name _____

Organization _____

Address _____

City _____

State/Province _____ ZIP/Postal Code _____

Telephone (   ) _____

Method of Payment:

☐ Enclosed is my check or money order

☐ Please charge to:

   ☐ MasterCard   ☐ VISA   ☐ American Express

Signature _____ Exp. Date _____

Credit Card Number

☐ ☐ ☐ ☐ ☐ ☐ ☐ ☐ ☐ ☐ ☐ ☐

To order multiple copies for co-workers and friends:	U.S.	Can.
20-50 copies	$8.50	$10.95
More than 50 copies	$7.50	$ 9.95

OTHER DESKTOP HANDBOOKS

Qty	Item#	Title	U.S.	Can.	Total
LEADERSHIP					
	410	The Supervisor's Handbook	$12.95	$14.95	
	418	Total Quality Management	$12.95	$14.95	
	421	Change: Coping with Tomorrow Today	$12.95	$14.95	
	459	Techniques of Successful Delegation	$12.95	$14.95	
	463	Powerful Leadership Skills for Women	$12.95	$14.95	
	494	Team-Building	$12.95	$14.95	
	495	How to Manage Conflict	$12.95	$14.95	
	469	Peak Performance	$12.95	$14.95	
COMMUNICATION					
	413	Dynamic Communication Skills for Women	$12.95	$14.95	
	414	The Write Stuff: *A Style Manual for Effective Business Writing*	$12.95	$14.95	
	417	Listen Up: *Hear What's Really Being Said*	$12.95	$14.95	
	442	Assertiveness: *Get What You Want Without Being Pushy*	$12.95	$14.95	
	460	Techniques to Improve Your Writing Skills	$12.95	$14.95	
	461	Powerful Presentation Skills	$12.95	$14.95	
	482	Techniques of Effective Telephone Communication	$12.95	$14.95	
	485	Personal Negotiating Skills	$12.95	$14.95	
	488	Customer Service: *The Key to Winning Lifetime Customers*	$12.95	$14.95	
	498	How to Manage Your Boss	$12.95	$14.95	
PRODUCTIVITY					
	411	Getting Things Done: *An Achiever's Guide to Time Management*	$12.95	$14.95	
	443	A New Attitude	$12.95	$14.95	
	468	Understanding the Bottom Line: *Finance for the Non-Financial Manager*	$12.95	$14.95	
	483	Successful Sales Strategies: *A Woman's Perspective*	$12.95	$14.95	
	489	Doing Business Over the Phone: *Telemarketing for the '90s*	$12.95	$14.95	
	496	Motivation & Goal-Setting: *The Keys to Achieving Success*	$12.95	$14.95	
LIFESTYLE					
	415	Balancing Career & Family: *Overcoming the Superwoman Syndrome*	$12.95	$14.95	
	416	Real Men Don't Vacuum	$12.95	$14.95	
	464	Self-Esteem: *The Power to Be Your Best*	$12.95	$14.95	
	484	The Stress Management Handbook	$12.95	$14.95	
	486	Parenting: *Ward & June Don't Live Here Anymore*	$12.95	$14.95	
	487	How to Get the Job You Want	$12.95	$14.95	

SALES TAX
All purchases subject to state and local sales tax. Questions? Call
1-800-258-7248

	Total
Subtotal	
Sales Tax **(Add appropriate state and local tax)**	
Shipping and Handling **($1 one item; 50¢ each additional item)**	
Total	